WAHINE WARRIOR

*From the ashes of trauma
emerges forgiveness and love.*

LOSA PATTERSON

Wahine Warrior: From the ashes of trauma emerges forgiveness and love.
Losa Patterson

First published in Australia © 2024 Losa Patterson

All rights reserved.

The author asserts the moral right to be identified as the author of this work.

No part of this book may be reproduced, stored in a retrieval system, or transmitted in any form or by any means—electronic, mechanical, photocopying, recording, or otherwise—without the prior written permission of the author, except for brief quotations used for review purposes.

ISBN paperback Interactive Edition 978-1-7636001-3-3
ISBN paperback 978-1-7636001-0-2
ISBN hardcover 978-1-7636001-2-6
ISBN ebook 978-1-7636001-1-9

Cover design & diagrams: Isaac Westerlund, Beckon Creative
Editor: Anne Hamilton
Interior typeset & design: Beckon Creative

 A catalogue record for this book is available from the National Library of Australia

This book presents information in a straightforward and accessible way, free from heavy academic jargon or extensive clinical research, which contributes to its appeal. It aims to deepen understanding and enrich experiences.

The languages and quotes featured in this book are designed to enrich cultural meaning and honour a variety of perspectives. Any inaccuracies or misinterpretations are unintentional and not meant to offend.

Before applying any insights from the book to well-being, it's important to consider their relevance to individual situations and seek professional guidance when needed.

ACKNOWLEDGEMENTS

In writing this book, I wish to acknowledge the traditional custodians of the land on which I live and work, the Dharug people. I pay my respects to their Elders, past, present, and emerging. I also extend this respect to all Aboriginal and Torres Strait Islander peoples across Australia.

I recognise the enduring connection that the Dharug people have to this land and the profound contributions of all First Nations peoples to our shared culture and community. Their wisdom in caring for the land inspires me deeply and informs my own understanding of harmony with the environment.

As a Pasifika woman working in trauma recovery, I am committed to healing and honouring the rich cultures and traditions of the Dharug people. I acknowledge the rightful place of all Aboriginal and Torres Strait Islander peoples as the First Nations of this land. May this acknowledgment be a step towards greater understanding, reconciliation, and collective healing.

As I prepared to speak at my mother's funeral, I asked myself what was the greatest gift she had given me. I knew immediately and had already manifested it when she was alive. What my mother has taught me is, *'Just as I breathe, I serve—I know no other way of life.'* I dedicate this book firstly to my mother for her service, sacrifice and unwavering faith.

In this book I share personal experiences, to embrace the past, empower the present and endure the future. I invite you all to be a new generation *Wahine Warrior* with a desire to heal and become AMAZING! With a prayer in my heart, I pray for all mother-daughter relationships to be precious and nurtured with a special sacred bond.

To my father whose humble beginnings began in Puipa'a, Upolu, Samoa. For all the challenges you conquered in life with your simple dreams and passions. Your relentless work ethic and sacred silence has been a powerful influence in my life.

I completed writing this book six months after my youngest sibling passed away. His departure impacted me more deeply than losing my parents. In his final months, we forged a deeper connection, mindful of the limited time we had left together. He expressed his love for me, and found joy in my accomplishments as his brother. His unwavering belief in me and encouragement inspired me to begin this writing journey. As we reminisced about our family memories, we acknowledged our differing perspectives and interpretations.

To my siblings, I express heartfelt gratitude for our shared past. While this book tells my story, I hold your stories close to my heart as well.

I dedicate this book to my children, grandchildren and my posterity. Motherhood has been my greatest learning tool in this life. Please forgive me for all the mistakes I've made, and there are many. You are all deeply imbedded in my heart. When I have passed away, beyond the veil, I will be so invested in every single one of you—make your lives wonderful!

To my beloved husband and best friend. Thank you for loving me unconditionally. You make my heart melt, and you make my heart swell. I know God loves me because He sent me you, a true source of healing in my life. I choose you always. What a blessing to spend eternity with you.

Finally, but not at all the least. I give thanks to Heavenly Father and Jesus Christ. With God nothing is impossible.

I am LOSA
and I am a
WAHINE WARRIOR!

Table of Contents

Introduction	11
Chapter 1: From the ashes, she emerged	13
Chapter 2: In my father's eyes	27
Chapter 3: Did you deserve it?	37
Chapter 4: I don't blame you; I blame your mother	49
Chapter 5: The drama triangle	59
Chapter 6: Unkept promises	73
Chapter 7: Love, heart, wisdom	85
Chapter 8: Beyond the veil	97
Chapter 9: I forgive you, please forgive me	111
Chapter 10: Be still and know that I AM	127
About the Author	139
Endorsements & Testimonials	141

INTRODUCTION

Over the years, it has been suggested that I write a book, especially by those who have heard about my life experiences. It seemed easy at first—just jotting down my life stories and the lessons learned. But it turned out to be more difficult than expected. The hardest part was reflecting on myself, doubting my capabilities, and worrying about how my writings might be received.

It is my hope that readers feel inspired and uplifted, finding courage and wisdom in my personal experiences and the insights gained. I pray that it is a positive and empowering reading experience, leaving you motivated and hopeful. Many people avoid thinking about the past because it can stir up painful memories. But General Bernard Montgomery, a wise figure from World War II, said something important: **'We need to understand our past before we can feel good about the future.'** His words have been spot-on for me as I've worked on this book.

For me, in each chapter there was an internal battle to put intimate encounters on paper, to share my vulnerability. However, my understanding was deepened, and I have become a better human being in the process. I have written this book like a therapeutic relationship; it allows the reader to interpret for themselves what they relate to and how they might help themselves become an expert in their personal healing journey. Ultimately the goal is to heal, not to stay stuck. To illuminate more desire and hope for good things in their life and create a life that is fulfilling and purposeful.

I don't consider myself extraordinary and I believe, if I can do it, you can do it! We all have stories that live inside us. To share them, understand them and rewrite them is phenomenal. I hope that my stories might resonate with your stories. I know that my transformation continues with excitement and joy. In my work and in my personal life, I aim to be the same person. Balancing professionalism with warmth and authenticity, my approach encompasses roles as a clinical psychotherapist, life coach, counsellor, mother, sister, and friend, where love trumps. Simply my message is:

I love you
I still love you
I will always love you

Why did I choose to call this book **Wahine Warrior**? I needed to be me, to express myself in my cultural context. I intentionally used different Pacific proverbs, to honour my Pasifika sisters, a sisterhood that we share from our beautiful Pacific *moana* (ocean).

From my heart to yours, I gift you this book with LOVE.

Alofa atu, Losa

"Ua logo i tino matagi lelei — Upu fiafia"
'A favourable wind is felt on the body — the joy of expectation'

Chapter 1:
From the ashes, she emerged

The preparations for a sea trip are complete. The travellers sit in the house and wait for the wind. Suddenly a gentle breeze is felt on the bare skin and by the direction it comes from — the people know that the weather is favourable. A wise Samoan proverb is: *'Ua logo i tino matagi lelei — Upu fiafia.'* Translated, it means: 'A *favourable wind is felt on the body — the joy of expectation'* and expresses my feelings that the time is right; the elements are in harmony for our journey ahead.

My name is Losa, pronounced *law-sah*, and this is where my story begins. I bear the name of my paternal grandmother, who passed away after giving birth to her twelfth child. With such a name, I carry not only her memory but also the rich tapestry of Samoa, my parents' homeland, heritage, and ancestry. My full name is Seilosa, pronounced *say-law-sah*. In Samoan, 'seilosa' can be interpreted as *beautiful rose*. The word 'sei' refers to a *flower worn behind the ear*, and 'losa' means *rose*. Combined, 'seilosa' conveys the idea of a rose being used as an adornment, highlighting its beauty.

Growing up I absolutely detested my name because I felt constantly ridiculed. People around me were unable to pronounce it correctly and as a child in a Eurocentric education setting, I was mocked and teased by both peers and teachers. Yet around mature Samoans, it was the opposite. In fact, my relations would throw themselves upon me, some sobbing in remembrance of my grandmother. A dichotomy of light and dark, kind and unkind, but a sure division within me because of my name. Neither of my parents explained who my namesake was, and why it was chosen.

Somehow, I knew that I was supposed to be a boy and to compensate and to appease my father, my mother named me after my paternal grandmother. In my thirties, I spoke to my mother, remarking that I was supposed to be a boy, wasn't I? And because I wasn't, you named me, Seilosa, after dad's mother.

She affirmed that it was true, so when I was in the womb, I was a child who was needed to counterbalance their marital tensions. In my mid-twenties, I was desperate to find more of my identity, so I approached my paternal aunt, who had known my grandmother. Learning about my grandmother's spirit and character made me appreciate my name for the first time. I really wish my parents had told me about her sooner.

My name caused me internal and emotional conflict, and my grandmother's early death caused trauma in my father's life. His unresolved trauma passed on to me, becoming intergenerational trauma that affected me. This burden might have been lessened if my parents had been more emotionally educated. Unfortunately, their lack of awareness extended to the depths of what they didn't understand. In this book, I share my personal stories and profound insights, shedding light on experiences and perspectives that may have been overlooked or misunderstood.

The gift of a name, which can sometimes feel like a curse rather than a blessing, is only one example of the complexities that come with inheriting a family legacy. It also highlights how often Polynesian names are mispronounced. You don't have to look too far to see how Pasifika names have not been pronounced correctly, respected, or honoured. It is only recently, particularly in the sports arena, attempts to rectify this issue are being addressed.

I am the fourth child who, for 12 years, was the youngest in my family of origin. Also, I was the only sibling to have a Samoan name — a unique distinction that made me stand out within my family and community. Growing up in the sixties, many Polynesian children were given Anglo-Saxon Christian names, helping them to fit in better at school. My own name seemed strange to others, and whenever teachers attempted to say it, it often turned into a humiliating experience. Their laughter and mockery made me dread the first day of school each year. Despite the cultural honour of being named after an ancestor, I felt marginalised and inadequate as a Samoan.

During my first university graduation, my teachers apologised for mispronouncing my name. Determined to reclaim my identity, I contacted the vice chancellor before my master's degree graduation and requested that my name be pronounced correctly during the ceremony. When my name was called, and I shook the vice chancellor's hand, he asked if they got it right. With a smile, I replied, 'Yes!'

My parents' relationship was tumultuous when I entered the world. At just four weeks old, we relocated from our first family home in Kingsland to dwell in a basement flat in Ponsonby, then later in Ranui, Auckland, New Zealand. In my first year of life, I experienced three different homes, residing with my parents and two sisters among paternal relatives in overcrowded conditions.

Though there were four children in our family, ranging from five years to myself as a newborn, my eldest brother primarily lived with our maternal grandparents. My father was recuperating from a significant financial setback, which led to our eviction. This event devastated my father and strained my parents' six-year marriage.

I have contemplated how different my life might have been if I had grown up in Kingsland —a community abundant with Samoan residents and schools with a significant Samoan population — compared to the sparse representation in Mt Roskill in the 1960s.

My father's consumption of alcohol escalated as he grappled with fear, shame, and betrayal. He had purchased his in-laws' property with cash, only to discover that the mortgage was in serious arrears. This deceitful act left him deeply wounded. In response, he began to distance himself from my maternal grandparents and the fa'a Samoa way of life, striving to reclaim his 'mana' and provide adequately for his family.

Born the son of a fisherman in a less affluent village than my mother's, my father was considered unworthy of my mother, but she was pregnant, and it was a shotgun wedding (and my father told me that my grandfather did indeed hold a shotgun to him). This perceived mismatch made their union vulnerable from the outset. In contrast, my mother, the 'golden child' of her family, was highly favoured by her parents.

Fluent and well-spoken in English with fair skin, she possessed qualities highly esteemed in a young Samoan woman. She was the first sibling to accompany her Samoan/Chinese father to New Zealand as a teenager. Initially, my mother went to Wellington to live with her aunt and assist with their catering business. Later, she joined her father in Tokoroa, where they worked as seasonal workers.

My father often recounted their love story to me, describing how they 'bit the apple' — a metaphor for my mother's pregnancy at the age of 17, with my father being seven years her senior. My mother's aspirations and the hopes of her family were abruptly shattered. Hastily, they were married off with the adage of 'they made their bed, now they must lie in it' —forever bound by the consequences of their actions. This was dictated by societal norms and familial expectations at that time.

I come from a culture where family is everything, family is first and without your family — you are nothing. As Figiel (1996) puts it, '*I* does not exist' because '*I* is always *we*.' Being Samoan also means believing in God. My ancestors marked the path for my religious affiliation. Some education professionals have inferred that my religious beliefs and practices were and are a part of colonisation. This suggestion — that my ancestors were ignorant and unable to discern secular knowledge versus spiritual experience — has frustrated me.

My childhood was marked by adversity. Our home was frequently tense, marred by domestic violence and alcohol abuse, particularly on paydays and weekends. These formative years, crucial for my development, were fraught with trauma and instability, creating inner conflict and turmoil that manifested in my behaviour.

Growing up as a minority in a predominantly white community had its struggles. Being 'brown' among mostly fair-skinned peers made me feel different and sometimes ashamed of my cultural background. I remember feeling self-conscious when my mum dropped me off at school in her fluorescent ultra plus-sized Polynesian dress styles.

Unfortunately, racism was a reality I had to deal with at a young age. Discrimination, both obvious and subtle, followed me from childhood into adulthood. It's difficult to forget the hurtful moments, like the stares and comments about my appearance compared to my classmates. Despite it all, I've learned to be resilient. These experiences have shaped me, but they don't define me.

My ancestors were keenly aware of the advantages associated with white privilege. While completing my genogram assignment for my master's degree, I researched the impact of marrying into the white diaspora. It was a common practice, to marry 'white' spouses in pursuit of higher social status and a better standard of living, or at least the perception of it.

An example of this was when my maternal grandfather and his siblings urged their father to change their Chinese surname to an English one, in the hopes of securing government jobs. Initially resistant, my great-grandfather eventually agreed to his children's wishes. The decision to relinquish their surname in exchange for better opportunities seemed insignificant and a small sacrifice at the time.

However, on reflection, it's important to consider what else may have been lost in the process and what price our family has paid as a result. The pursuit for movement that minimises disparity often comes with its own set of complexities and consequences, prompting us to examine the true cost of assimilation and societal acceptance.

I refuse to continue the cycle of intergenerational pain. My journey of healing and growth is filled with divine purpose. I willingly shoulder the burden so that my descendants may learn in the light, free from the shadows of the past. I choose love, so that kindness, gratitude, and safety will surround my posterity. Each morning, I try to embrace joy, refusing to squander precious time on self-sabotage and resentment. Forgiveness is the means to genuine healing. Through my journey, I've come to understand that forgiveness is not a single act but an ongoing process, continuously evolving and unfolding over time.

Writing this book has stirred up a multitude of feelings and reactions that have led to a deeper understanding of myself. Initially, when faced with overwhelming emotions, my instinct was to avoid and procrastinate. To run away and disconnect, which was then followed by an onslaught of self-sabotage thoughts, doubting my worth and capabilities.

With each chapter I've found myself on a voyage on the Pacific Ocean. Sometimes, it's like standing on the shore, basking in the sun's warmth, and feeling the gentle sea breeze, embracing the beauty of the moment. Other times, it's like diving into the waves, seeking renewal and vitality in the deep blue waters. Yet, there are moments when I'm unexpectedly caught in a rip tide, fighting against the relentless pull of turbulent waters, desperately struggling to stay afloat, grasp onto stability, and regain my balance amidst the stormy currents of life. Most of the people I work with are

Pacific Islanders. I feel honoured and privileged to journey with them. For this purpose, I have used Pasifika language and quotes to honour them and weaving their 'mana' into my script.

In Māori culture, 'mana' is of profound significance, embodying a fusion of spiritual potency, esteem, and authority. Central to this concept is the belief that all individuals are inherently endowed with mana from birth, signifying a universal possession of this special energy. Mana serves as a marker of one's influence and prestige within the community, intricately intertwined with ancestral lineage, cultural traditions, and the natural environment. Consequently, mana holds a pivotal role in Māori identity, encapsulating their worldview and societal values.

Recollecting my stories brings remembrance, and re-visiting. I've selected experiences that I felt would be helpful. I have not written consecutively in a scripted timeline. In fact, as a reader you can read any chapter out of sequence and resonate with it. In my tsunami of emotions, I've navigated these metaphorical waters with greater resilience and purpose. I've embraced vulnerability, allowing myself to float, paddle, and swim while ensuring I never allow myself to drown. With newfound meaning and determination, I feel as though I have a new reservoir of strength and vitality like being reborn as a **new generation Wahine Warrior!**

With a fresher perspective and a deeper understanding of myself, I approach life with a renewed sense of purpose. I've gained a new set of metaphorical 'safety goggles', allowing me to see things from a different angle and explore new avenues of growth and healing. I've learned to reframe my narrative, finding solace and inspiration in even the most challenging moments.

If trauma has often felt like a dark and relentless force in your life, you can overcome the shadows of your past and emerge as a warrior, ready to embrace your divine purpose and destiny with an open heart and unwavering determination.

Ensuring your safety as a reader is paramount. Picture if you can, that you are manuhiri, *a visitor*, waiting to come onto the marae, *the meeting place*. Imagine that you are engaged with the Pōwhiri process, *the welcome*, to enter the marae — a sacred special space. Let me walk you through the process:

1. **Wero (Challenge):**

    A male warrior or representative from the hosting group performs actions or gestures symbolising potential conflict. This is a symbolic way of testing the intentions of the visiting group.

1. **Karanga (Call of Welcome):**

    Following the challenge, a series of calls, known as karanga, *are exchanged between female members of both the hosting and visiting groups. This serves as a formal and ceremonial welcome, expressing hospitality and unity.*

1. **Whaikorero (Speeches):**

    Once the karanga is completed, speeches are given by male representatives from both the hosting and visiting groups. These speeches typically express gratitude, acknowledge the significance of the occasion, and establish connections between the groups.

1. **Waiata (Songs):**

    Throughout the pōwhiri, waiata (songs) are sung, often in response to speeches or as a form of expression and unity.

1. **Hongi (Pressing of Noses):**

   The pōwhiri culminates with the hongi, a traditional Māori greeting where individuals press their noses and foreheads together. This act symbolises the sharing of breath, and is a gesture of respect, connection, and unity between the hosts and guests.

Just as these steps collectively form the pōwhiri process, a ritualised protocol that honours Māori cultural traditions and values of hospitality, respect, and unity, I use this symbolism as I invite you into my book, my space, my stories, which will become our space, our stories, our experiences, our healing.

I present this Māori chant to provide you with support and comfort, to ensure your safety. I express gratitude for your bravery in engaging and relating to my book. Our collective narratives will strengthen, nurture, and empower us to embody the spirit of a *Wahine Warrior!*

'Kia ora, kia ora
He ora, he ora
He hā, he hā
He mauri, he mauri
Kia ngākau whakapai
Kia ngākau whakapai
Whakangaro i te tawhito
Whakatō i te oranga
Tipu, rea mō te whakaora
me te mātauranga,
Kia wahine toa!'

> '*Be well, be well*
> *It is life, it is life*
> *To breathe, to breathe*
> *To live, to live*
> *To have joy, to have joy,*
> *Bury the past, sow the seeds of new life,*
> *Grow, thrive, for healing and education,*
> *Be a warrior woman!*'

While I hold professional titles like clinical psychotherapist, trauma life coach, therapeutic specialist and mental health practitioner, in these pages, please be with me, simply as Losa, a daughter, sister, wife, mother, aunty, grandmother, and friend.

Reference:

Figiel, S, (1996). *Where we once belonged*. Auckland: Pasifika Press

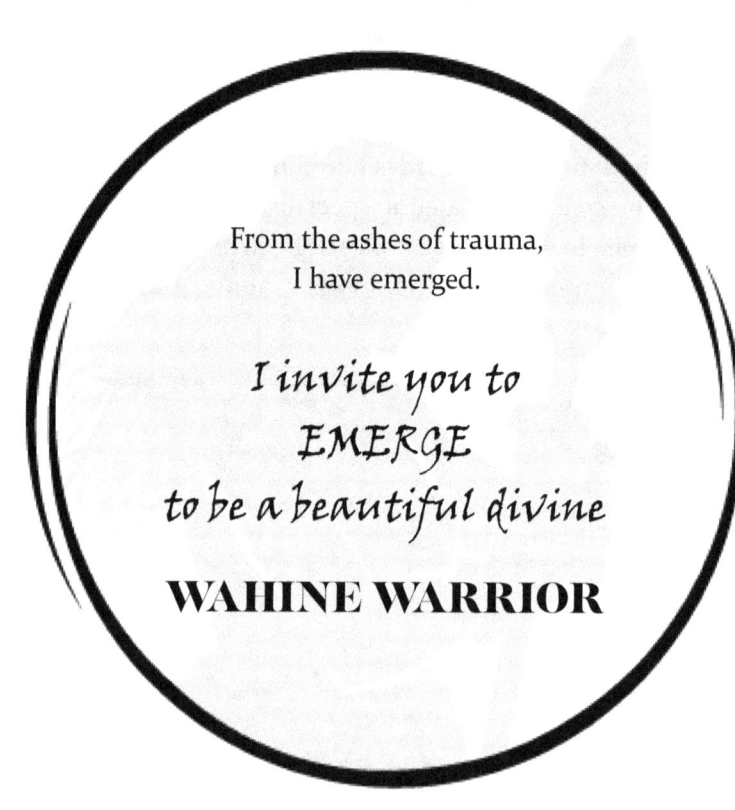

From the ashes of trauma,
I have emerged.

I invite you to
EMERGE
to be a beautiful divine
WAHINE WARRIOR

Definitions:

Mana

From a Māori perspective, mana is a deeply significant concept that encompasses authority, power, and spiritual essence. It's an integral part of Māori culture and identity. Here are some key aspects:

1. **Spiritual Power:** Mana is seen as a supernatural force that is inherited from ancestors, and it can be enhanced or diminished by one's actions and deeds.

2. **Authority and Influence:** It reflects a person's standing, influence, and leadership within the community. Those with high mana are respected and have a significant role in decision-making and guidance.

3. **Respect and Honour:** Maintaining and enhancing one's mana involves living according to cultural values, demonstrating respect for others, and contributing positively to the community.

4. **Connection to Land and Ancestors:** Mana is also connected to whenua, *the land*, and whakapapa, *one's lineage*. It emphasises the relationship between people, their ancestors, and the natural world.

In essence, mana is a multifaceted concept that intertwines power, respect, spirituality, and responsibility, forming a core part of Māori cultural and social structure.

Pōwhiri

A pōwhiri is a traditional Māori welcoming ceremony. It involves a series of steps to greet and show respect to visitors.

*'Mo te faiva foki ki te mafola,
mo te mamae foki ki te olaga.'*
'For the warrior embraces the challenge in his soul
and endures the pain.'

Chapter 2:
In my father's eyes

I walked into Oakley hospital to the acute psychiatric ward, and saw my father restrained in a straight-jacket, his upper body immobilised for fear he would harm himself or others. He was in a locked padded room — isolated, fragile, and vulnerable. As I looked into his eyes, it was as if I looked into his soul. Immediately I thought, *'I know that my father was a lot of things, but he is not this — he is no animal.'* In my father's eyes, I saw what I describe as 'Betrayal Trauma.'

My dad was born and raised in the village of Puipa'a, located in the paradise of Apia, Samoa. He had 14 siblings, 3 who died at infancy. My father faced a challenging childhood. His older brother was deaf and mute, and due to this disability, he was designated to accompany my grandfather on their fishing expeditions at sea. They would set out early in the morning to retrieve the nets and bring in their catch. When my uncle couldn't join, this responsibility often fell to my father, becoming a regular occurrence.

Growing up my father's main duty was to sell the fish before heading off to school. This was challenging for him, as he would then attempt to do his homework while riding his bike on the way to school. Once my dad returned home from school, his time was fully occupied with endless chores, especially tending to the garden and plantation around the home. Severe consequences awaited my father at school, if he fell asleep in class or his homework was not completed. However, he did his utmost to avoid such retribution. English was his worst subject, but he loved mathematics.

His job of selling his father's fish taught him how to count his earnings and generate profit. This was the work experience that motivated dad to save his fare to leave Samoa and move to New Zealand. Dad was the village lender. Frequently, the men in his village would find themselves short of money just before payday, so they would turn to my father to borrow cash. My father charged them interest, and they typically repaid him within 1-2 days. Dad would pick the sugar cane that fell off the trucks and sell the stalks. With his entrepreneurial skills, he saved enough money to migrate to New Zealand on his own.

Tragedy came into my father's life when he was only 12 years old. His mother passed away due to complications during childbirth. This affected him immensely and, due to there being so many children, he was sent to live with his cousins to lighten his father's load. I share my father's growing up years, so that you can get a sense of him — a native Samoan hard-working boy, who came to New Zealand in search of a better life at the age of 19. Despite having limited English and resources, he had the courage and independence to move abroad. Upon arriving in New Zealand, he enrolled in night school, worked in factories, and eventually embarked on a carpentry apprenticeship — the career path he chose. Five years later, at the age of 24, my father married my mother.

Fast-forwarding to my father's situation as an inpatient at the Oakley Psychiatric Hospital, he is 57 years old. He is retired, the family home in Central Auckland is where he, my mother and my younger brother live. There is a tiny mortgage that he pays off at $25.00 per month. His marriage was like a war-and-peace movie, but mostly war. Despite the hardships he has endured, he finds contentment in his life now, savouring his homemade brew, enjoying the fruits of his labour, and able to retire comfortably — to him, life is good.

Myself, I am 28 years old, residing in West Auckland. My morning was underway, my two eldest daughters had already departed for school. At home, I am caring for my young baby, and the phone rings (before the time of cell phones and internet). My mother's voice, strained and distressed, begged me to hurry over, citing an urgent matter. Initially, my mind raced through potential dramas she might have embroiled herself in. Cynically, I ask her, 'What have you done now?' With emotions overflowing she revealed that the police were on their way to take my father.

I bundled up my baby, speed-driving to my parents' home. I arrived in time to witness my father being handcuffed and escorted to the backseat of a police car. His expression was one of desolation, tinged with shame and sheepishness. Completely caught off-guard, he offered no resistance, accepting the situation without protest. My father had always steered clear of law enforcement encounters, with no prior criminal record to speak of.

Jump ahead two weeks from my father's admission to the acute psychiatric ward. He has now been discharged, thanks in part to a capable lawyer who not only understood my father's broken English but also grasped the intricacies of his situation. Through legal manoeuvring, the allegation made by my mother — that my father's mental health state was a threat to himself and to the community — was overturned, and my father was released to return home. My mother had signed my father under the mental health act, declaring in an affidavit that he was at risk of taking his own life. I was gobsmacked and without words, when I realised what my mother had done. For my father, this was the last straw. From that time onwards, he separated from my mother.

Taking up residence in the garage, my father physically distanced himself from the marriage. The car garage was not a comfortable setup; it lacked the amenities of a typical living space. With its cold, unlined walls, and concrete floor, it offered a roof, but not warmth. Despite their already estranged relationship, my father's move to the garage marked a definitive separation. His boundaries were an implicit statement that he would no longer trust her. When my father was drunk, he would always say to me, 'Your mother is after my money, she wants the house and the money.'

Amidst this mayhem, my father worked closely with his lawyer to safeguard assets. He drafted a matrimonial settlement for my mother to sign, placed the family home in a trust for the children, and then purchased a new property before leaving. With his careful savings, he bought a new home and returned to work to pay off the mortgage within a year. Once that was accomplished, he retired again, continuing his frugal lifestyle and saving money each week.

A self-taught accumulator, my father was meticulous with his finances. He avoided extravagance, conserving resources wherever possible. His prudent habits contradicted the stereotype of an alcoholic, let alone a suicidal mental health consumer. While some children yearn for their parents to reconcile, my deepest wish since childhood had been for their separation. I longed for a household free from constant conflict, where peace could finally reign.

As I reflect on my mother's actions, I can't help but consider that her decision to sign an affidavit may have stemmed from her desire to escape the unhappiness of her marriage. In a society where separation or divorce was stigmatised, she wanted to save face, and avoid the label of a failed marriage. She could claim that she was a victim, preserving her perceived reputation. Witnessing her actions filled me with a profound sense of disbelief and moral repulsion.

At that time as an adult, I found myself overwhelmed with intense anger, but I would go into survivor mode and numb my feelings as a coping mechanism. Thankfully I had my own family that I needed to focus on, and I established firm boundaries with my mother to shield myself from further emotional manipulation and turmoil.

In hindsight, I realise that I inadvertently distanced myself from understanding my mother's perspective and empathising with her struggles. Burdened by my own unresolved trauma, I unintentionally erected barriers that hindered our relationship, thus preventing me from offering her the support she may have needed. On reflection, I don't think I had the psychological stamina and flexibility to embrace my mother's personality.

These complex dynamics of trauma, betrayal, and manipulation are my identified lessons that can now be a koha, a *gift*, to you as my reader. The gift to understand, embrace the past, to release it and heal:

1. **Emotional Manipulation:**

    My mother's actions, such as signing an affidavit to declare my father as mentally impaired, suggest a form of emotional manipulation aimed at achieving her own goals, including gaining possession of their property. This manipulation can involve exploiting vulnerabilities or using emotional tactics to control or influence others.

2. **Gaslighting:**

    Gaslighting is a form of psychological manipulation where an individual seeks to make another person doubt their own perceptions, memories, or sanity. In this case, my mother may have been attempting to portray my father as mentally impaired — potentially causing him to question his own mental state or the validity of his actions.

3. **Trauma Inflicted on Others:**

    My father may have experienced significant emotional trauma because of being falsely labelled as mentally impaired, especially if this false characterisation had led to legal or social consequences. Being accused of posing a risk to himself and others could have had profound effects on his self-esteem, sense of identity, and relationships.

4. **Betrayal Trauma:**

    If my father trusted my mother and believed that she had his best interests at heart, discovering that she signed an affidavit to declare him as mentally impaired could be deeply traumatic. This sense of betrayal can shatter trust and lead to feelings of anger, hurt, and disillusionment.

5. **Family Dynamics:**

    The manipulation and trauma described in this situation can also have broader impacts on family dynamics and relationships. It may lead to feelings of division, resentment, and mistrust among family members. It can also strain existing bonds and exacerbate conflicts.

6. **Legal and Financial Consequences:**

    Beyond the emotional trauma, there may be legal and financial ramifications from my mother's actions, including potential legal proceedings or disputes over property ownership. These consequences can further complicate and exacerbate the emotional toll of the situation.

This real-life situation had a complex interplay of manipulation, emotional trauma, and legal consequences. Empathy, understanding, and a willingness to seek support from trusted individuals or professionals, was required. My father received good legal advice which served him well. Counselling was not a service that my parents valued or engaged in — not even pastoral support. In fact, I remember my mother receiving wise counsel, not only from church ministers but also from an uncle, encouraging her to make changes in the home for the sake of the children.

At the time I was bewildered by what my mother did, and I judged her harshly for it. Now, understanding, releasing, and healing are invaluable gifts.

As the Tuvaluan proverb affirms: 'Mo te faiva foki ki te mafola, mo te mamae foki ki te olaga.' *Translated it means:* 'For the warrior embraces the challenge in his soul and endures the pain.'

A
WAHINE WARRIOR
*endures pain
with faith and courage.*

She faces challenges with courage
while acknowledging the importance
of enduring pain as part of the journey
toward healing and growth.

Definitions:

Koha

The Māori word koha refers to a gift, offering, or contribution. It is often given as a sign of respect, gratitude, and reciprocity. Koha can take many forms, such as food, money, or handmade items, and is commonly presented during gatherings, ceremonies, or when visiting someone's home. The act of giving koha is an important cultural practice that strengthens relationships and acknowledges the value of hospitality and support.

*'Na dina ni sautu, na kaukauwa ni bati,
na loloma ni yalo.'*

'The truth of resilience, the strength of endurance,
the love of the heart.'

Chapter 3:
Did you deserve it?

Feeling like a beached whale, I was visiting with my parents, trying to pass time in my final trimester of pregnancy. I was expecting my first child, also the first grandchild for my parents. Hanging around familiar settings was comforting as I was transitioning from childhood into adulthood with responsibilities of becoming a mother. Married for 5 months, with only 5 weeks till my baby's arrival, I felt like I was navigating uncharted territory.

Naïve, young without guile, I was optimistic about life, but nervous of the unknown. I was living one day at a time, without a vision for the future. Being so large with child I felt so off-kilter, wobbling around, trying not to bump into the furniture. Just getting up out of a chair required careful calculated effort. I had never encountered so many changes in my body while having so little emotional awareness. Looking back, I often found myself disconnected from my body, a common experience for those raised with trauma, as denial had been my go-to response.

As an 18-year-old girl facing an unplanned pregnancy, I was overwhelmed by a mix of emotions. Fear, uncertainty and a profound sense of responsibility. The idea of becoming a mother at such a young age felt surreal, like a plot twist in a story I never imagined for myself. I wasn't living at home, and the place where I stayed wasn't ideal. My parents' relationship remained unchanged — they shared the same roof but love and kindness between them were rare occurrences. My mother conveyed that they couldn't accommodate me without inconvenience, yet I yearned for their love and nurturing.

Pre-natal hospital visits, ultrasound scans, kick counting, blood tests, screenings, pelvic examinations and birth planning was my life. I found myself going home for respite and relaxation. I didn't drive and relied heavily on my mother to be my taxi driver. Our mother-daughter relationship was closer as I looked to her for guidance and assurance. I was becoming a mother, even though I was still a child myself. Frequenting my family home with my parents was a way to stay connected, avoid feeling alone and anxious while waiting for my baby to be born. Little did I know how much my life would change simply by becoming a mother.

I was embracing the warmth of the sun on my back as I leaned against the dining room window at my parents' house. My father was getting ready to go out when the rumblings of an argument started. This was very familiar; I'd seen it for years; it was like a repeat episode of a soap opera drama. During their heated argument, both parties exchanged verbal attacks filled with contempt and demeaning remarks, mixing English and Samoan to inflict pain and undermine each other. I'd witnessed these episodes my entire life.

The circling began, the chase through the kitchen, hallway, lounge then the dining area. The red flag signalling that something will soon be hurled, and the likelihood of physical violence would break out. As a young child I had strategies to endure these scenes, and not once did I intervene but today was different. Tired and fed up I screamed at them both, 'For goodness' sake, I am bringing a child into this world, your first grandchild, just STOP!'

I had many colourful words in my head, but a Samoan daughter would never disrespect her parents with foul language, even when they used vulgarity towards each other. Taking deep breaths, holding my belly, I screamed, 'Enough! That is enough!!!' Such was my chastisement of them.

Reflecting on that pivotal moment, I realise that I birthed a new version of myself — a Wahine Warrior, fiercely asserting my boundaries and demanding respect. When I screamed at them, 'Enough! That is enough!!!', a wave of empowerment surged through me, forcing me to take a stand against the toxic dynamics that had plagued our family for years.

The shock on my parents' faces was palpable as my words pierced through the tension-filled air. In that moment, the power dynamics shifted. My father, perhaps feeling the weight of conviction, chose to retreat, escaping the confrontation by driving away. Meanwhile, my mother, unable to face me, sought refuge somewhere within the confines of our home.

Though our silence on the matter remained, the impact of that encounter stayed within me long after the echoes of our heated exchange faded. It was a turning point — a catalyst for change. From that day forward, I found the courage to stand up and challenge my parents, refusing to be silenced or cower in the face of adversity. I embraced my role as a Wahine Warrior, determined to assert my autonomy and reclaim control over my own life.

Sadly, my young married life disintegrated rapidly. Emotional and physical abuse from my spouse appeared and began repeating itself more. Technically I was the victim, but I knew we were both victims because we both had trauma and abuse backgrounds. The odds had always been against us. I regretted complying to be married. The attempt to right the wrong of our immorality was not a wise corrective action. We were both so young without the skills and knowledge to become a happy healthy family. The occasion when my then-husband grabbed hold of my 3-year-old and held her hostage throughout the night was a defining moment — an intergenerational episode of *Enough! That is enough!!!*

My innocent helpless child was sobbing with fear and looking at me to rescue her, but each time I tried to retrieve her, he threatened to harm her. It was the longest night of my life. Early that morning, when he had fallen asleep, I quickly took my two children and left, never to return or reconcile into that abusive relationship. Married for only 3 years, at 21 years young, I endured two occasions of adultery, his pornography addiction and domestic violence. I packed my things and went home.

I hadn't told my mother what was happening, or how miserable, lonely, and unhappy I was. Mustering up the courage, I told my mother that I had been getting beaten, and the first words to come out of her mouth were, 'Did you deserve it?'

That was not the reaction I expected, but sadly, I was not surprised. I wasn't invited back or welcomed home, and I did not return to my marriage. My mother wanted me to reconcile with my spouse, as having a separated or divorced child was considered more shameful. A caring minister at the time warned me that my mother would always want to save face. I was more determined because, deep down, I knew I didn't deserve it. I resented my mother for a long time for not being there for me. I felt dismissed, unloved, and unseen. Looking back, let's analyse my mother's mindset:

When a mother encourages her daughter to return to an abusive and violent marriage, it often stems from her own unresolved trauma and complex emotional dynamics. Here are some factors that may contribute to this behaviour:

1. **Normalisation of Abuse:**

    If the mother herself experienced abuse in her own relationships, she may have normalised or minimised the severity of abuse. This normalisation can lead her to believe that enduring abuse is inevitable or acceptable in a marriage.

2. **Survival Mode:**

    The mother may have developed coping mechanisms to survive in her own abusive relationship, such as denial, rationalisation, or avoidance. As a result, she may struggle to recognise the full extent of the danger and harm her daughter is facing.

3. **Fear of Change:**

    Leaving an abusive relationship can be incredibly challenging and fraught with uncertainty. The mother may fear the unknown and worry about the practical and emotional implications of her daughter leaving the marriage, such as financial instability or social stigma.

4. **Protecting the Family Unit:**

   The mother may prioritise maintaining the family unit and avoiding societal judgment over prioritising her daughter's safety and well-being. She may believe that keeping the family together is more important than addressing the abuse.

5. **Limited Resources and Support:**

   The mother may feel overwhelmed by the prospect of supporting her daughter through leaving the marriage and may lack the resources or support network to assist her effectively.

6. **Guilt and Shame:**

   The mother may experience feelings of guilt or shame for not being able to protect her daughter from the abuse or for her own perceived failures in the relationship. This guilt and shame may manifest as a desire to downplay or dismiss the severity of the abuse.

7. **Trauma Bonding:**

   If the mother has experienced trauma bonding in her own abusive relationship, she may struggle to recognise or break free from the cycle of abuse. This can lead her to inadvertently perpetuate the cycle by encouraging her daughter to stay in the abusive marriage.

8. **Cultural and Societal Influences:**

   Cultural and societal norms around marriage, gender roles, and family dynamics can also play a significant role in shaping the mother's beliefs and attitudes towards abuse and marriage.

It's been important for me to have empathy and understanding, recognising that my mother's actions were driven by her own unresolved trauma and complex emotional dynamics. In my attempts to try to have open communication with strategies and supports to help her, she was offended and felt I was condescending, believing she was 'fine' and that her belief in God was enough. When a person isn't ready, you cannot force or coerce them to be. To think you just remove or eliminate the trauma is not enough, you must replace it with the opposite to become whole.

Addressing and healing from trauma is a multifaceted process that involves replacing the negative effects of trauma with positive experiences and emotions to foster healing and wholeness. This can include creating a sense of safety, cultivating feelings of happiness, peace, and love, and building resilience to future challenges. By replacing the trauma with positive experiences and emotions, individuals can work towards reclaiming their sense of self and restoring balance in their lives.

In my first marriage where emotional and physical abuse was present, it was crucial to prioritise safety and well-being above all else. My identified lessons I offer to you as a koha, a gift, to you, the reader. The gift to understand your mana, your courage and strength to act:

1. **Seek Help:**

    Seeking professional help is valuable, but it must be of high quality. Be aware that not all practitioners may be suitable for you, particularly in terms of cultural humility and cultural competency. Pastoral support from trusted ministers might also be more accessible and affordable. Both partners can seek individual therapy to address their past traumas and develop healthy coping mechanisms. Additionally, couples therapy can provide a safe space to explore relationship dynamics and work towards healthier communication and conflict resolution.

2. **Safety Planning:**

    If physical abuse is involved, it's essential for the abused partner to create a safety plan. This may involve identifying safe places to go in case of an emergency, keeping important documents and belongings in a secure location, and having a trusted person to reach out to for support.

3. **Set Boundaries:**

    Establish clear boundaries with the abusive partner regarding acceptable behaviour. Clearly communicate what behaviours are unacceptable and the consequences for violating those boundaries. Consistently enforce these boundaries to protect your well-being.

4. **Address Addiction:**

    If the husband has an alcohol, drug, gambling, or pornography addiction, both partners should seek support to address this issue. This may involve individual therapy, support groups, or addiction counselling to address the underlying issues contributing to the addiction.

5. **Support Networks:**

   Surround yourself with a strong support network of friends, family, and professionals who can offer emotional support and practical assistance. Joining support groups for survivors of abuse can also provide validation, understanding, and encouragement.

6. **Legal Protection:**

   If necessary, seek legal assistance to explore options for obtaining a protection order or restraining order against the abusive partner. Legal protection can provide an added layer of security and enforce consequences for abusive behaviour.

7. **Self-Care:**

   Prioritise self-care practices to nurture your physical, emotional, and mental well-being. This may include engaging in activities you enjoy, practising relaxation techniques, and prioritising your health and safety.

8. **Make Informed Decisions:**

   The decision to stay in or leave an abusive relationship is deeply personal and complex. Educate yourself about the dynamics of abuse, explore your options, and make decisions that prioritise your safety, well-being, and long-term happiness.

In my specific circumstances, I decided to leave the marriage due to ongoing abuse and a toxic environment reminiscent of my parents' marriage. My decision to prioritise my own well-being was driven more for the well-being of my children. It was crucial to keep them safe. I remembered how I felt as a child and how broken and unsafe I felt growing up.

The Fijian proverb, *'Na dina ni sautu, na kaukauwa ni bati, na loloma ni yalo,'* translated means: *'The truth of resilience, the strength of endurance, the love of the heart.'* It acknowledges the journey of overcoming adversity with fortitude and love.

A

WAHINE WARRIOR

*embodies resilience,
endurance, and compassion.*

She will rise above challenges
and inspire others with her
courage and kindness.

*'Fakalofa lahi atu ki he laumanu,
fakalofa lahi atu ki he tānaki.'*
'Love deeply for the wounded, love deeply for the healer.'

Chapter 4:
I don't blame you; I blame your mother

On an ordinary day at our family home, despite my parents being separated, my father remained a constant presence. He could always be found tending to the garden, lost in his own world, pottering about in his outdoor sanctuary. Before sitting down for his 'smoko'—a cherished term he used—he'd typically carry his thermos flask and packed lunch. His grandchildren often followed him, mimicking his every move and eagerly waiting for the moment he would share his 'smoko' with them.

On this particular day, I had interrupted the pleasant bonding time my father was enjoying with my daughter. In a harsh, authoritarian tone, I was summoning her to hurry up and come to me. Sensing my hostility, my father approached me, his eyes piercing into my soul as he sought to shield his granddaughter from the emotional stress I was about to inflict. In his broken English, he said, '*Losa, put your voice down, don't yell at the child. I don't blame you, I blame your mother — you are only doing what your mother did to you.*'

His heartfelt words tugged at my emotions, conveying his love, kindness, and earnest plea to mend both his past mistakes in parenting and those of my mother. It felt as though a heavy burden had been lifted, granting me the freedom to break away from the cycle of history repeating itself. This transformative experience was truly life-changing for me.

A few short stories highlighting valuable lessons I learned from my father:

Caught Smoking!

Despite never having hit me, my father instilled a fear in me that surpassed anything my mother could evoke. I vividly recall the day I was caught smoking. My mother informed my father, and I braced myself for the worst. He approached me, holding the packet of cigarettes, and posed a challenge: smoke the entire pack in front of him. I hesitated, unwilling to comply.

Instead of resorting to punishment, my father shared a personal story. He recounted his own experience with smoking, how he had quit after watching a documentary on its detrimental health effects. He warned me of the dangers, particularly the link to cancer and death. Then, he offered an ultimatum: Either he disciplines me with the water hose to deter me from smoking, or I find an alternative.

Quickly realising the gravity of the situation, I declined his offer. I made a solemn vow never to smoke again. It was a promise I've steadfastly kept, never lighting another cigarette since. Reflecting, I realise the profound influence my father had on me, even in my adolescent years when I didn't fully appreciate it. As a teenager my father's wisdom and guidance didn't resonate with me fully, but as I've grown older, they've guided me towards a safer path, shaping me for the better.

Kneeling before him to confess

At seventeen, I found myself walking the same path as my mother when I became pregnant. The most daunting aspect of it all was facing my father. My mother made it clear that it was my responsibility to tell him; she wouldn't do it for me. With a heavy heart, I approached him, adhering to the traditional Samoan gesture of kneeling down and bowing my head in shame.

I confessed my situation, bracing myself for his reaction. His initial response was one of anger and disappointment. He demanded that I leave the house immediately and never return. I obeyed, feeling the weight of his words heavy on my shoulders. However, after a few agonising days, I mustered the courage to return home.

Once again, I knelt before my father, expressing my sincere remorse. This time, tears flowed freely from both of us. In that moment of vulnerability, he softened, allowing me back into the fold. It was a moment of forgiveness and reconciliation, marked by tears of both sorrow and relief.

Sacred Silence

Following an emergency caesarean delivery, I welcomed my second child into the world. During my recovery, my father made his customary visit, but this time his behaviour showed that he was more affected than usual. Upon entering my room, his expression shifted to one of grave concern as he beheld my condition. I was still undergoing a blood transfusion and tethered to various machines, a sight that unsettled him deeply.

Contrary to his normal practice of visiting the hospital once, my father began coming to see me every day. Each time, he would greet me with a tender kiss on my forehead, inquire about my well-being, and engage in light conversation. Then, without uttering a word, he would simply sit by my side for an hour or two. In those sacred silent moments, I gleaned profound insights into my father's inner world.

I learned of the grief and pain he had carried with him throughout his life. His own mother had tragically passed away when he was young, succumbing to complications from childbirth. I felt the weight of his trauma, but I also sensed a healing presence emanating from him. In those sacred moments we shared, amidst the beeping of machines and the sterile hospital environment, a profound connection blossomed between us, forged through unspoken understanding and shared vulnerability. As a natural consequence, my dad also formed a special attachment and bond to that grandchild, an added blessing.

Feeling Safe

Leaving my marriage took a lot of courage, and telling my parents required just as much. Initially held back by the fear of confiding in them, I eventually summoned the strength to take that step. At that time, my parents were still together, albeit in a strained relationship, which meant I had to approach them separately. I told my mother, but for some reason, I couldn't bring myself to tell my father.

As time passed, I sensed that my father had become aware of my situation. One day, he came over to my place to tend to my lawn and hedges. When I went out to offer him a cold drink, he broached the subject with a simple question: 'So, how long does it take to get a divorce?'

I replied, 'Two years.' He nodded in understanding before quietly continuing with his tasks. And with that brief exchange, he said all he needed to say on the matter. I felt respected, loved and seen. My father was a man of few words, but the feeling of safety made his words more profound, effectively influencing not only my life but my children's.

My daughters chuckle as they reminisce about a cherished tradition. Grandpa would buy them their own packet of fish and chips, wrapped in nostalgic, grease-stained paper. They would poke a hole in the top corner of the paper pack, eagerly reaching in to enjoy their favourite grandpa treat, savouring the crispy, salty aroma. He would then drive across the road to the local pub — all within a 5-minute trip from the family home. While they sat and ate their soul food, my dad would quickly go to enjoy his pint at the pub. Wonderful memories arise with the aroma of takeaway chips. My children recall that even in the carpark at the pub, they always felt safe with Grandpa.

A short story with my mother that troubled me, even as an adult

I was thirteen years old and found myself once again in trouble with my mother, though I can't recall the exact reason. With my mother, trouble seemed to follow me wherever I went, and I could never do anything right. As we stood in the hallway, tensions escalating, she reached for her weapon of choice: the metal pipe from the vacuum cleaner. I recall thinking to myself: 'Are you kidding, you're really going to do this? I'm not a little kid anymore, in fact I am taller and stronger than you. I can outrun you effortlessly!'

In a split second, as she raised the pipe to strike me, something inside me snapped. Instinctively, I grabbed hold of it, breaking her grip, and wrestled it away from her. In that moment, a surge of anger and violence coursed through me. I entertained thoughts of retaliating, of using the pipe against her. But as quickly as the impulse arose, I recoiled in horror at the thought of harming my own mother.

Instead, I threw the pipe to the ground and fled. It was the first time I ran away from home, propelled by a mixture of shock, fear, and self-loathing. The realisation that I had entertained thoughts of violence against my mother shook me to the core. It felt like I was staring into a dark abyss, glimpsing the potential to become the very thing I despised: an abuser.

To analyse myself, I understand that my thoughts of retaliation were informed by trauma; I was mirroring what had been done to me. Instead of becoming a perpetrator, I chose to run away. It wasn't until my adult years that my father's words lifted a heavy weight I had carried: 'I don't blame you; I blame your mother.' His words were and still are a lifeline — a release from the suffocating grip of abuse that had trapped me for so long.

Now, as I have embarked on the journey of healing and more self-discovery, my koha, or *gift*, is this treatment plan to my 13-year-old self:

1. **Addressing Intergenerational Trauma:**

    I understand that my experiences are not isolated but are part of a larger cycle of trauma within my family. Therapy should delve into this intergenerational pattern to help me break free from its grasp.

2. **Exploring Violent Impulses:**

    It's crucial for me to unpack the violent impulses that surfaced during the altercation with my mother. Therapy will provide a safe space for me to explore the origins of these impulses and develop healthier coping mechanisms.

3. **Navigating Self-Blame and Forgiveness:**

    I need support in navigating feelings of guilt and shame, as well as in cultivating self-compassion and forgiveness. Therapy will help me reframe my self-perception and embrace a more positive outlook.

4. **Family Dynamics:**

    Family therapy will be instrumental in addressing dysfunctional dynamics and fostering healthier communication and relationships within my family unit.

5. **Trauma Recovery:**

   With the guidance of trauma-focused therapy, I aim to process past traumas, develop effective coping strategies, and build resilience in the face of adversity.

6. **Cognitive Behavioural Techniques:**

   Incorporating cognitive-behavioural techniques will empower me to challenge negative thought patterns, manage anger, and develop alternative responses to conflict.

7. **Psychoeducation:**

   I'm eager to learn more about the cycle of abuse, the impact of trauma on behaviour, and strategies for fostering healthy relationships. Psychoeducation will equip me with the knowledge and skills needed to navigate my journey toward healing.

8. **Safety Planning:**

   Given the potential for further conflict and violence in the home, developing a safety plan is paramount to ensuring my physical and emotional well-being. This plan will involve identifying safe spaces, establishing emergency contacts, and implementing coping strategies for managing crisis situations.

As the protagonist of my own story, speaking to my 13-year-old self feels like addressing my wounded shadow — a companion that has followed me into adulthood. Exploring these shadow values has been crucial in understanding my true priorities and bringing them into conscious awareness. A 'shadow value' refers to those deeply held values that may not be openly acknowledged or expressed. Often unconscious or hidden, they contrast with the values one publicly upholds.

Reflecting on the past to rewrite my story, reinterpret that script, understand it, release it, and heal, I'm committed to breaking free from the cycle of abuse and reclaiming control over my narrative. With the right support and resources, I believe I can emerge from this ordeal stronger, wiser, and more resilient than ever before. Oh, how I wish that my family and I had received the help we needed back then, to get on the healing path sooner.

The Niuean proverb at the beginning of this chapter, 'Fakalofa lahi atu ki he laumanu, fakalofa lahi atu ki he tānaki,' when translated, means: 'Love deeply for the wounded, love deeply for the healer.' Emphasised is the importance of love and compassion in both supporting those who have experienced trauma and acknowledging the strength and resilience of those who help in the healing process.

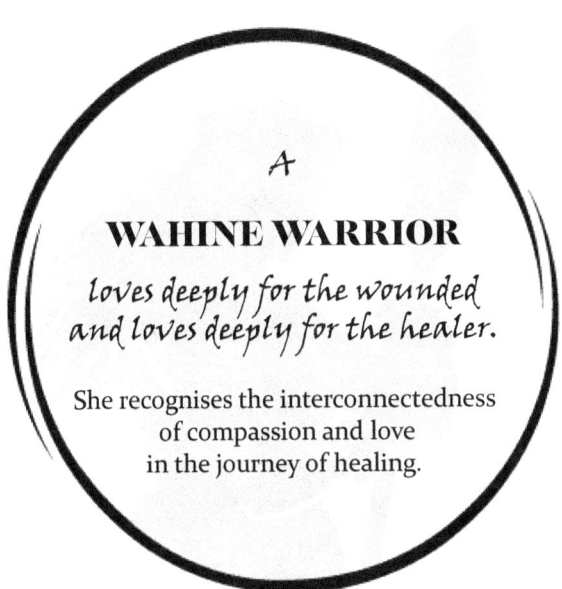

A
WAHINE WARRIOR
loves deeply for the wounded and loves deeply for the healer.

She recognises the interconnectedness
of compassion and love
in the journey of healing.

*'Kia manuia te tere o te moana,
kia atinga te kauvai ora.'*

'May the journey across the ocean be smooth,
may you reach the source of living water.'

Chapter 5:
The drama triangle

I was barely a teenager when my siblings and I gathered in my mother's workshop to have a conversation. This setting felt unfamiliar, as we rarely discussed our family circumstances. It often seemed like we were enduring rather than confronting what was happening. During this meeting, my older brother, though still quite young himself, made a profound statement that has stuck with me. He simply said, 'Mum is depressed.'

I struggled to comprehend depression; my empathy and connection with my mother were lacking. I was familiar with my father's life experiences because he often shared stories from his upbringing, particularly the challenges he faced. However, my understanding of my mother's childhood was limited. Unlike my father, she didn't readily share her past. Yet, I suspect my older brother knew more about it, as he spent his formative years under the care of our maternal grandparents.

I found it peculiar that I had no recollection of my older brother from my early years, so I decided to ask my mother about it. She clarified that he had been living with her parents, hence his absence from our home. Her own words were: 'It was like World War III when I asked for your brother to return home to live with us.'

Despite her pleas, her mother adamantly refused to send him back home. It was a relentless battle for her to secure his return and, when he was school age, she seized the opportunity of schooling as a pretext for his homecoming. The experience must have been profoundly heart-wrenching — having to plead and humble herself for the return of her own child.

I find myself contemplating the dynamics between my maternal grandmother and my mother. When my brother transitioned to living with us, my grandparents only allowed him to stay on weekdays, taking him back every weekend. My mother disclosed that her parents would wait nearby, anticipating his tears and longing for them, so they could swoop in and take him back. These covert actions clearly demonstrated their disregard for my mother's wishes and feelings, prioritising their own needs above hers.

My mother undoubtedly grieved for her first born. As a young and vulnerable new mother, she faced the heart-wrenching reality of her parents claiming him as their own, usurping her role. Reclaiming him was a hard-fought battle. During his formative years, he was enveloped in love, cherished by his adoring grandparents who lavished attention on him as their first grandchild. It was a markedly different beginning to life from my own.

When my maternal grandmother passed away overseas, my mother attended the funeral, and upon her return, my father confided in me that she had seemed to adopt her mother's persona. In sharing this observation, he also revealed his own sense of loss regarding his wife. I couldn't help but wonder if, amidst her grief, my mother felt burdened by guilt or shame, leading her to embody aspects of her mother's personality. It's a curious shift that prompts me to ponder its underlying issues.

Drama frequently surfaced in my relationship with my mother and, although labelling her a 'drama queen' may not be the kindest approach, it did provide me with insight into the drama triangle. I liken my mother-daughter dynamics to the mysterious Bermuda Triangle, since I often felt lost within our relationship. This reflection has also highlighted how I can become entangled or play a similar role in my other relationships.

The drama triangle is like a game where people play different roles: the victim, the rescuer, and the persecutor. The victim feels powerless and blames others for their problems, while the rescuer tries to fix things and take control. The persecutor blames the victim and criticises them. Sometimes people switch roles, but the game usually ends up causing more problems than it solves. Breaking out of the drama triangle means taking responsibility for our actions and finding healthier ways to deal with conflicts.

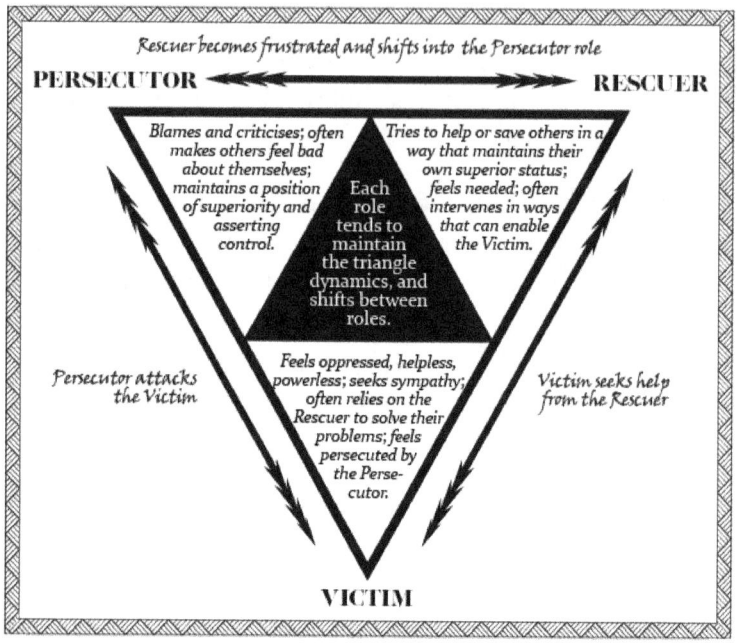

The Bermuda Triangle, also known as the Devil's Triangle, is famous for the mysterious disappearances of ships and planes. It has fascinated people for a long time. Similarly, the Bermuda Triangle is a good metaphor for the complexities of trauma and abuse in relationships. Just as vessels get lost in the ocean's vastness, people caught in the drama triangle can feel lost and powerless during conflict and manipulation.

In the drama triangle, **the persecutor role often mirrors the unseen forces at play in the Bermuda Triangle** — a looming, ominous presence that instils fear and uncertainty. Victims of abuse may find themselves navigating treacherous waters, constantly on edge and bracing for the next wave of aggression. The persecutor's tactics of intimidation, control, and coercion create a sense of helplessness and vulnerability, leaving victims feeling as though they are adrift in a sea of chaos.

In my marriage, there are times when I feel relatively okay, but then something small triggers me, and I become annoyed. It could be as simple as walking into the kitchen to find unwashed dishes while my family is happily spending time together in the lounge. In that moment, a barrage of negative thoughts floods my mind — they're ungrateful, I'm always the one doing everything, and I feel entitled to express my frustration through yelling and criticism.

Like the Bermuda Triangle metaphor, I become like a looming, ominous presence, instilling fear and uncertainty in my family. I realise that my unresolved trauma is driving this behaviour, causing me to repeat patterns of intimidation and control that I learned from my own upbringing. This behaviour emerges especially when things are calm at home, as if I'm trying to disrupt the peace because I don't know how to handle it.

Can anyone relate to this experience?

To overcome and resolve this persecutor role within the drama triangle, I recognise that I need to address my unresolved trauma and the underlying emotions that trigger my negative reactions. This may involve seeking therapy or support to process and heal from past experiences. I also need to learn healthier ways to communicate and manage my emotions, instead of resorting to tactics of intimidation and control. By taking responsibility for my actions and actively working towards personal growth and change, I can break free from the cycle of negativity and create a more harmonious environment within my family.

Conversely, **the victim role in the drama triangle reflects the plight of those lost in the Bermuda Triangle** — overwhelmed by a sense of powerlessness and resignation. Victims of abuse may internalise feelings of guilt, shame, and self-blame, convinced that they somehow deserve their mistreatment. Like ships at the mercy of the elements, they may feel powerless to escape the cycle of abuse, resigned to their fate.

In my line of work, I often encounter people who fall into the victim role by catastrophising, which means they perceive situations as much worse than what they are. This behaviour is common when someone is stressed or anxious, and I've experienced it personally.

For instance, consider a typical scenario in my life. My husband is usually very attentive, but sometimes he gets caught up with work and doesn't text me or answer my calls right away. When this happens, my mind tends to jump to the worst possible conclusions. Instead of thinking that he might simply be busy, and his phone is on silent, I start to believe that he doesn't care about me or our relationship. I worry that he might be losing interest in me, or that he's avoiding me for some reason.

As these thoughts spiral, my anxiety increases. I might start to feel neglected and unimportant, and these feelings can build up throughout the day. By the time I finally get to speak to him, I'm already upset. Instead of calmly asking him why he didn't respond, I might accuse him of not being committed to our relationship. I could say things like, 'Why didn't you answer my calls? Don't you care about me anymore?'

My husband, taken by surprise and likely feeling attacked, might respond defensively. He might say something like, 'I was just busy at work! Why do you always assume the worst?' This defensive reaction can make me feel even more upset and unsupported, reinforcing my negative thoughts.

In the heat of the moment, I might threaten to separate or even mention divorce. These threats are a result of feeling hopeless and overwhelmed, believing that the situation can't improve. This reactive pattern is what we call learned helplessness — when someone feels so stuck in a negative cycle that they start to believe there's no way out, leading them to make drastic decisions.

This kind of catastrophising can be very damaging to relationships. To truly overcome the victim role and break free from the drama triangle, individuals may need to seek support and guidance to address their underlying trauma and develop healthier coping mechanisms. This may involve therapy, counselling, or other forms of self-care and personal growth. By reclaiming their sense of agency and taking proactive steps to address their needs and boundaries, individuals can empower themselves to create healthier, more fulfilling relationships in the future.

Meanwhile, **the rescuer role in the drama triangle mirrors the efforts of search and rescue teams tasked with locating missing vessels in the Bermuda Triangle** — driven by a desire to save others from harm, even at their own expense. Rescuers may become enmeshed in the drama triangle, sacrificing their own well-being to alleviate the suffering of others. Yet, despite their best efforts, they may find themselves pulled deeper into the cycle of dysfunction, unable to break free from its powerful undertow.

I am a recovering yeller and I cringe now at how I have yelled! My mother was a yeller, and I found myself repeating the pattern. One day, my young child asked me why I was so mean to daddy. This honest question made me realise I needed to understand and change my behaviour.

Instead of justifying my actions, I explored my emotions and past experiences to find the root causes of my anger and frustration. I discovered my yelling stemmed from stress, unresolved trauma, and poor coping mechanisms. I learned healthier ways to manage my emotions and communicate with my family. My relationship with my husband has improved, and I'm setting a better example for my child. It's an ongoing journey, but I am committed to breaking the cycle of yelling and fostering a nurturing, supportive family environment.

Unfortunately, I have also trained my child to be a rescuer, just as I was growing up. Children who grow up in such environments often take on rescue roles beyond their years, becoming parentified and forced to take on responsibilities they shouldn't have to bear. They become hyper-aware of potential conflict, always trying to prevent a major blow-up. And as they grow older, they may struggle to form healthy relationships, still carrying the scars of their upbringing.

To break free from this cycle, it requires deep introspection and soul work, but the transformation is worth it. The rescue role in the drama triangle can suffocate you in later years to reject authentic good relationships. It is more than people-pleasing dynamics, it is unresolved trauma — another way of saying it is trauma-informed behaviour seen in children, youth and adults.

Do you know anyone who seems to be incredibly helpful and caring outside of their own home, but with their family, they act completely differently? It's like they're wearing a mask, pretending to be someone they're not. Take, for example, a person who is quick to support others in need but struggles to recognise or address their own problems.

Think about a situation where a father sacrifices everything to help his extended family, leaving his own family struggling to survive. It's like he's neglecting his own needs to fulfill the needs of others, even when it's at the expense of his own family's well-being.

This behaviour reflects the dynamics of a rescuer in the drama triangle. Rescuers often prioritise helping others at their own expense, sometimes to the point of neglecting their own needs. Just like the safety drill on an aircraft where we're reminded to put on our own oxygen masks before helping others, it's crucial for rescuers to prioritise self-care and recognise when they need support themselves.

At its core, the drama triangle is a model that describes dysfunctional interaction patterns within relationships, involving three primary roles: **the persecutor, the victim, and the rescuer**. These roles perpetuate a cycle of conflict, blame, and disempowerment, often leading to emotional turmoil and distress for all involved. Similarly, the Bermuda Triangle can be seen as a metaphorical representation of the drama triangle, highlighting the complexities and dangers inherent in dysfunctional dynamics.

Identifying your own participation in the drama triangle within any type of relationship—whether with a spouse, romantic partner, family members, close friends, colleagues, sports teammates, or acquaintances—requires self-awareness and introspection. Here are some signs that you may be initiating or perpetuating drama triangle dynamics:

1. **Assuming the Persecutor Role:**

   You may find yourself criticising, blaming, or controlling others in ways that mirror the persecutor role. This can include using harsh language, making unfair accusations, or resorting to manipulation to assert control in any relationship, including with a spouse or romantic partner.

2. **Adopting the Victim Role:**

   Conversely, you might portray yourself as the victim, seeking sympathy or validation from others by emphasising your own suffering or helplessness. This could involve playing the martyr or exaggerating your hardships to elicit a desired response from a spouse, romantic partner, family members, or close friends.

3. **Rescuer Behaviour:**

   You may engage in rescuer behaviour by attempting to 'fix' or 'save' others from their problems or challenges. This can manifest as overstepping boundaries, enabling unhealthy behaviour, or taking on responsibilities that are not yours to bear in various relational contexts, including with a spouse or romantic partner.

4. **Engaging in Manipulative Tactics:**

   You might resort to manipulative tactics to control others' emotions or behaviour, such as guilt-tripping, gaslighting, or withholding affection or support as a form of punishment. This can occur in any relationship, including with family members, close friends, or colleagues.

5. **Avoiding Accountability:**

   You may resist taking responsibility for your own actions or behaviours, deflecting blame onto others or external circumstances instead. This can create a cycle of defensiveness and denial that perpetuates conflict and undermines trust in any relationship, including with a spouse, romantic partner, or colleagues.

6. **Repeating Unhealthy Patterns:**

   You may find yourself repeating patterns of behaviour or communication that mirror those from past experiences or relationships. This can include using similar language, adopting similar roles, or reacting in ways that are familiar but ultimately unproductive in all types of relationships.

7. **Feeling Stuck in Conflict:**

   You might feel stuck in a cycle of conflict or tension with others, unable to break free from destructive patterns of interaction. This can create a sense of frustration, resentment, or despair that undermines the health of any relationship, including those with a spouse, romantic partner, or sports teammates.

Recognising these patterns is the first step towards breaking free from the drama triangle and fostering healthier dynamics in your relationships. By cultivating self-awareness, practising effective communication, and seeking support when needed, you can work towards building a relationship based on mutual respect, empathy, and trust.

'*Kia manuia te tere o te moana, kia atinga te kauvai ora*' translated means '*May the journey across the ocean be smooth, may you reach the source of living water.*' This Cook Islands proverb conveys wishes for a safe and prosperous journey, both literally and metaphorically and emphasises the importance of reaching a source of sustenance and vitality.

References:

Karpman, S. (1968). Fairy tales and script drama analysis. *Transactional Analysis Bulletin*, 7(26), 39-43.

Berlitz, C. (1974). *The Bermuda Triangle*. New York: Doubleday.

A
WAHINE WARRIOR
has relationships that provide nourishment, energy, and a sense of fulfillment.

She seeks spiritual sustenance
that refreshes and renews,
leading to inner growth
and transformation.

'Talo tadau moana, gulea ma'o.'
'Rise like the ocean wave, resilient and strong.'

Chapter 6
Unkept promises

My mother was a striking figure — an obese, large, fair-skinned Samoan woman whose presence commanded attention. In the chaotic year of 1977, I felt emotionally lost, struggling with overwhelming inner turmoil. I was a ripe fifteen-year-old, filled with hope as I embraced my adolescence. Turning sixteen later that year was something I eagerly anticipated, despite the whirlwind of hormones and awkward moments that came with it.

During one especially distressing moment, my mother's behaviour reflected my own inner chaos. Like a toddler throwing a tantrum, she rolled her morbidly plus-sized body on the ground kicking with her feet and hands, uttering the words that she wished I had died because my behaviour was so unacceptable. It was a moment of profound pain for me, and I really felt worthless. I hated my life and had little desire to be alive. 1977 was one of the darkest chapters of my teenage years.

As I reflect on that desolate season of my juvenile life, I can't help but wonder how different things might have been if circumstances had been kinder. It's easy to pinpoint 1979 — the year I became pregnant — but the catalyst for my struggles was in the seeds of turmoil sown earlier. The wounds inflicted in 1977 festered and bled into the subsequent years, shaping tough experiences and choices during those pivotal teen years.

The vision of attending our family's church boarding school held great hope for me. My three older siblings had already had this privilege, and it was finally my turn. It was a family tradition and my expectation — a promise from my mother that I would be able to fulfil my dream in 1977. With excitement bubbling within me I eagerly inquired about registration and uniform purchases and was told that I couldn't attend because of financial hardship.

I was absolutely shattered. The devastation was overwhelming, compounded by feelings of dismissal and inferiority, especially when I compared myself to my siblings who had gone before me. While I wasn't fully conscious of the depth of my hurt at the time, I distinctly remember feeling betrayed. I was being denied, despite my years of hard work in the home, helping with my mother's business, cleaning, baking banana cakes to sell, endless babysitting for my younger brother and the many tasks, sacrifices and service I contributed to the home.

Looking back to my 15-year-old self, I find myself overwhelmed with anguish as I reflect on the events that transpired. It's a pivotal time that altered the course of my life forever — a pain point that remains vivid even now. I grappled with an absent mother who remained oblivious to the turmoil brewing within me. In hindsight, the impact of that rejection on my psyche was profound, shaping my outlook on life and relationships in ways I'm only now beginning to fully understand. I find myself wrestling with questions that have long haunted me: *Why didn't you see me? Why didn't you care? Why didn't you keep your promises?*

Would my life have been different if my mother kept her promise? I was still a 'good girl' trying my best.

I was always described as clingy, a sook and a brat. Even recently, in my sixties, my aunties have spoken of me in that way. That stigma and their attitude towards me has been hurtful and unkind; I still feel their dislike and disdain for me.

One example was when we gathered for a family reunion. I was in my forties. I had travelled for nine hours on a plane, arrived at the campsite and as I greeted my aunt with a kiss, the first words she uttered were: 'Oh, you're so fat!'

My response was, 'And I love you too.' The culture I grew up in often involved mocking and belittling, which felt demeaning and contrary to the values we upheld. Although our family was known for its strong religious beliefs, my experience sometimes felt disconnected from the compassion and kindness I associate with Christian values, both as a child and as an adult.

Their lack of emotional intelligence and ignorance of brain health reflects the family's intergenerational trauma that remained untreated. My undiagnosed ADHD (attention deficit hyperactivity disorder) was interpreted as rebellion and disobedience from infancy. I recall my 9-month-old child crawling on my mother's kitchen floor, pulling out the pots and pans as an adventure activity. My mother told me how defiant she was in her learning from play experience. Shaking my head with disappointment, I responded, 'Mum, she's only 9 months old, she doesn't even know how to be defiant. She is just playing with pots and pans, she's only a baby.' This scenario recalls the way my mother and her sisters saw me as a child growing up.

Starting school at age 5, I was assigned a speech therapist due to a learning deficit, as I struggled with correctly pronouncing words and often said and wrote them out of sequence. At home my father's pidgin English was often not properly ordered and he would say things like: 'Pick your mouth up from the ground.' As a child, I observed unkind behaviour associated with the Samoan language spoken by my parents, which led me to form a negative perception of it. This association, coupled with my own experiences of anxiety and early onset of dysthymia (mild chronic depression), contributed to my reluctance to engage with the language. My understanding of the language became intertwined with these negative emotions, impacting my ability to connect with it.

I didn't like school, and, in those primary years, every report card amplified the fact that I was not able to concentrate and focus. I still remember always gazing out the window, using my vivid imagination, letting my mind tour to adventures instead of the mundane boring classroom. In my forties, while at university, three of my professors inquired if I had dyslexia. I realised that anxiety can sometimes present in ways that resemble dyslexia in a classroom setting. As an adult, I found myself triggered, reflecting my childhood experiences within a Eurocentric education system where I often didn't feel culturally safe as a minority. This situation also brought out trauma-informed behaviours rooted in my upbringing. Like many Polynesian children, physical education was my favourite subject and I excelled in netball. Netball saved my life at primary and intermediate school!

Developmental stages, particularly the critical formative years from birth to age three, are often regarded as the blueprint for your personality, cognitive abilities, and emotional development. If developmental milestones from birth to age three aren't successfully reached, it can impact various aspects of development later in life, including cognitive, emotional, and social functioning.

At 15 years old, I faced academic struggles, emotional dysregulation, social difficulties, and behavioural issues, all rooted in my early childhood experiences. The encouraging news is that despite not reaching developmental milestones, these deficits can be repaired; neuroplasticity enables us to achieve that. *Don't ever think it's too late to heal from trauma and improve brain health* — it's entirely achievable!

Here are some tips for nurturing emotional connection between a mother and child, even if there wasn't a strong bond from birth to fifteen — in fact, these strategies can be used for any age:

1. **Start Small:**

    Begin by spending quality time together in activities that your child enjoys, even if it's just a few minutes each day. Focus on building positive experiences and memories.

2. **Express Love and Affection:**

   Show your child love and affection through words, hugs, and gestures of care. Let them know that you value and appreciate them.

3. **Listen Actively:**

   Practise active listening when your child talks, showing genuine interest in their thoughts, feelings, and experiences. Validate their emotions and provide empathetic responses.

4. **Be Patient:**

   Building a strong emotional bond takes time and patience. Be patient with yourself and your child as you work to strengthen your relationship.

5. **Seek Professional Support:**

   Consider seeking guidance from a therapist or counsellor who specialises in family dynamics and relationships. A professional can offer insights and strategies to help repair and strengthen the emotional bond between you and your child. *For Pasifika children, youth, and adults, culturally competent services are essential. Research indicates that services designed 'for Pacific, by Pacific' are considered best practice.

6. **Create Opportunities for Connection:**

   Find opportunities to spend quality time together, such as going for walks, cooking together, or engaging in shared hobbies or interests. These shared experiences can help deepen your emotional connection.

7. **Practice Forgiveness:**

    Let go of past hurts and resentments, focusing instead on building a positive future together. Practise forgiveness and compassion, both for yourself and your child.

8. **Communicate Openly:**

    Foster open and honest communication with your child, encouraging them to express their thoughts, feelings, and concerns without fear of judgment or criticism. Be willing to listen and understand their perspective.

9. **Celebrate Progress:**

    Acknowledge and celebrate the progress you make together, no matter how small. Recognise and appreciate the efforts you both put into strengthening your relationship.

10. **Stay Consistent:**

    Be consistent in your efforts to connect with your child emotionally, even during challenging times. Your consistency and commitment will help build trust and stability in your relationship.

Remember that building a strong emotional bond is an ongoing process that requires effort and commitment from both parties. By taking proactive steps to nurture your relationship, you can create a stronger, more resilient bond with your child (no matter what age), even if it didn't develop as strongly as you would have liked in the past.

Writing has helped me to delve deeply into the complexities of my relationship with my mother, a connection fraught with tension and unspoken resentments. The recent passing of my brother has brought these dynamics to the forefront. It is April 2024, just five months since the death of my youngest brother, the first and only sibling to have passed away.

In the final days of my brother's life, he expressed a longing to be reunited with our mother. His words stirred within me a sense of envy — not jealousy, but a realisation that I didn't share his sentiments. In fact, since her passing, I've found a sense of relief and peace, as if the noise of her disapproval had finally quieted.

I've long sensed that my mother struggled to connect with me, to affirm me in the way a mother should. Despite following her path of early marriage and motherhood, and later battling obesity to eventually to become healthier and slimmer in my late forties, her approval remained elusive. Instead of acknowledging my achievements, she expressed jealousy and resentment, lamenting that she should have been the one to transform, not me. Ironically, she had lost weight, which was such an incredible achievement, but she was unable to sustain the change.

It often felt as though nothing I did could please her, leaving me perpetually cast as the scapegoat in our strained relationship. I couldn't help but wonder if her animosity toward me was fuelled by my close bond with my father and I tried to understand what was in me that triggered her. She constantly complained even about my father's visits to my home for family dinners. These times enhanced his relationship with me and my children, but her moaning about it to my dad eventually meant that he stopped coming. I was hurt that my mother would sabotage healthy, endearing relationships.

Sadly, my mother's bias against me extended to my children, evident through her clear favouritism. One Christmas, my children received nothing more than a cheap packet of peanut slabs, accompanied by a promise note that she would sew them an outfit—a promise that, like many others, remained unfulfilled. In stark contrast, their cousins were showered with more expensive gifts that conveyed her genuine affection and thoughtfulness, such as duvets, blankets, and toys.

This behaviour was not just disappointing but deeply hurtful, affecting both me and my children. It created a painful pattern of unkept promises and inequitable treatment that was passed down to the next generation. To shield ourselves from the emotional damage and protect our well-being, we distanced ourselves from her, emotionally insulating ourselves as if against a fatal disease.

It's evident to me now that my mother's struggles to connect with me were deeply rooted in her own unresolved trauma. Throughout my upbringing, her actions and attitudes seemed to reflect the unhealed wounds of her past, which she unwittingly projected onto me.

1. **Unresolved Trauma:**

   My mother's upbringing likely left her with unresolved trauma that coloured her interactions with me. Perhaps she experienced hardships or trauma in her own childhood that she never fully processed or addressed.

2. **Emotional Instability:**

   Her emotional instability, manifested in behaviours like tantrums and hurtful remarks, suggested a deep-seated struggle to manage her own emotions. This instability likely made it difficult for her to provide the nurturing and support that I needed as her child.

3. **Limited Coping Skills:**

   Without the necessary coping skills to address her own emotional wounds, my mother may have inadvertently lashed out or withdrawn when faced with challenging situations or emotions, further hindering our ability to connect.

4. **Interpersonal Dynamics:**

   Our strained relationship may also have been influenced by broader family dynamics or cultural expectations that shaped her views on motherhood and familial relationships.

5. **Projection:**

   In projecting her own unresolved trauma onto me, my mother may have unknowingly transferred her pain and insecurities, exacerbating the disconnect between us.

Recognising these factors has helped me understand the complexities of my mother-daughter relationship and provided insight into the challenges we faced in connecting with one another. Like the Solomon Islands proverb, *'Talo tadau moana, gulea ma'o,'* I will *'Rise like the ocean wave, resilient and strong.'*

A
WAHINE WARRIOR
perseveres and emerges stronger from life's challenges.

She likens herself to the Pacific Ocean
and rises with resilience and strength.

*'Fakakaukau ke tauhi e 'ofa,
ke tauhi e loto, mo e maama'a.'*

'Be prepared to embrace **love**,
embrace the **heart**, and embrace **wisdom**.'

Chapter 7:
Love, heart, wisdom

Years ago, a gathering of Pacific women united for a research venture centred on trauma and abuse. I count myself fortunate to have been part of this assembly, composed of resilient and accomplished Pacific professionals. Among us were devoted mothers, employed and esteemed within our communities. Some were married, others single, yet all shared a bond of mutual respect and support.

Over nine months, we convened regularly with two professors, one male and one female, who, though not Pasifika themselves, displayed a genuine desire to comprehend our Pacific heritage. Their cultural integrity earned our trust as they grasped our ways, nuances, and meanings. In our sessions, we traversed a spectrum of emotions — laughter, tears, and profound introspection. Together, we dissected our lives, selves, and community contexts. It was a thorough and transformative journey, infused with love, heart, and wisdom.

Amidst our shared narratives, we found solace in collective resilience and unwavering solidarity. We identified intergenerational patterns — both strengths and weaknesses inherited from our ancestors. Some of us drew parallels with biblical texts, envisioning the Abrahamic covenant and its foresight into future struggles.

Upon completion of the project, as we prepared for publication, we unanimously decided against its release. The fear of being recognised by our parents, despite anonymity, overshadowed our willingness to share deeply personal and often dark stories. Nonetheless, we expressed sincere gratitude for the transformative power of the group therapy we had received.

Our healing journey was guided by potent 'talanoa', *storytelling*, and the exchange of experiences. Rituals like prayer, poetry, song, and communal meals played pivotal roles in our recovery. As participants, we not only received healing but also acted as experts, supporting one another through the process. Though the facilitators were university professors, their non-Pasifika background did not hinder the cultural safety we felt. Each of us, as Pasifika women, embodied values of compassion, kindness, and love — key components for healing. It was a deeply spiritual experience. Our emotional intelligence increased, our resilience was strengthened, and our spirits intertwined. In a spirit of sisterhood, we were individually and collectively Wahine Warriors and as we left the room each session, our heads were held higher.

Choosing not to publish our stories of trauma and abuse was the correct decision for us at that period of time. We used wisdom. Now, in this current phase of my life, the courage to share through my writings feels akin to a responsibility. To refrain from sharing would leave me with a regret I am unwilling to bear. My approach to sharing is rooted in preserving dignity and enhancing mana, and there is never an intention to cause harm through my words.

For the remainder of this chapter, I will emphasise the importance of love, heart, and wisdom, fundamental elements of embodying the spirit of a Wahine Warrior!

A Wahine Warrior embraces LOVE

Our group was receptive and eager to both receive and give love. Raised with a cultural ethos of service and ministry, love and service were intertwined in our upbringing. In this group, it was easier to love — compared to a setting where familial dynamics involved triggers that could lead to regression into past conflicts.

In my family we had been raised as Christians and, at my parents' funerals, we were tested in our sibling relationships. I had always thought our faith was strong, and in times of crisis that we would unite. If we had differences, then we would put those differences aside and be more Christlike, because we knew that was the right way. However, that was not my experience. Sadly, at a time when we needed each other the most, there were misinterpretations, misunderstandings and power plays that divided us. In my mind, we mirrored out parents' dysfunctional relationship — with the drama triangle game playing at its best. Some of this was conscious and some unconscious, but always, there were trauma-informed behaviours.

We often rationalised saying that we loved each other, yet we failed to show kindness and empathy as a family. This has been one of the saddest seasons of my life. Is it possible to love when you don't forgive and hold onto resentments? What is really happening? Let's take a closer look into that. When someone says they love you but still harbours resentment, it indicates a complex emotional state. They may genuinely feel that they love you, but their inability to forgive and the fact they continue to hold grudges suggest unresolved issues or pain. For that person, there could be several underlying factors at play:

1. **Emotional Conflict:**

   They might be experiencing a conflict between their feelings of love and their unresolved hurt or anger towards you. This internal conflict can create confusion and inner turmoil.

2. **Fear of Vulnerability:**

   Forgiveness often requires vulnerability and letting go of protective emotional barriers. The person may fear being hurt again if they forgive or worry that forgiveness implies weakness.

3. **Lack of Closure:**

   The person may not have fully processed or addressed the underlying issues that led to the hurt or resentment. Without closure, it's challenging to move past negative emotions and truly forgive.

4. **Control Dynamics:**

   Holding onto resentment can sometimes be a way for individuals to maintain a sense of control or power in a relationship. They may use resentment as a means of asserting themselves or protecting their boundaries.

5. **Difficulty in Expressing Emotions:**

   Some people struggle to communicate their feelings effectively. They may express love to convey positive emotions while still finding it difficult to articulate their unresolved negative feelings.

6. **Unrealistic Expectations:**

   They may have unrealistic expectations of what forgiveness entails or believe that forgiveness means condoning the other person's actions. This misconception can hinder their ability to forgive.

Ultimately, when someone expresses love but simultaneously holds onto resentment, it indicates a need for deeper exploration and healing of their emotional wounds. It's essential for both parties to communicate openly and compassionately to address underlying issues and work towards reconciliation and forgiveness. Love conquers ALL — **LOVE is essential in being a Wahine Warrior!**

A Wahine Warrior Embraces the HEART

I recall a time when I was struggling with one of my daughters during her adolescent years. She didn't want to be with the family and, as a mother, I felt at a loss, not knowing what to do. I had a lightbulb moment and decided to ask my family for help. We gathered in our family home and, as I expressed my concerns about my daughter going astray and rebelling against us as parents, I was shocked by their hostile judgments and lack of support. I thought that they would embrace me with their hearts but instead I found myself in the firing line, being told that I was failing as a mother and unable to control my child. This was an example of them not listening with their heart. All but one sibling were critical of me, telling me that I just needed to discipline my child and that child should just be obedient — end of discussion.

I thought we were Christians, and I was expecting love, which was what I needed. I was hurt by the unkind and cold reception. I had more comfort and support from groups outside of my family — like my wonderful wahine group — than from my immediate family.

Embracing the heart was an integral experience within our trauma wahine group. We cherished emotional connections. It seemed effortless. Unlike siblings bonded by trauma, our women's group shared stories that nurtured rather than crippled us, shielding us from vicarious trauma. This contrasted starkly with my family relationships. Trauma bonding often blinds families affected by intergenerational trauma. Nurturing involves uplifting, fortifying, and empowering individuals to rise from the ashes of trauma. Here are some tips on how to nurture the heart and foster emotional connections:

1. **Practise Active Listening:**

    Show genuine interest in others' experiences by listening attentively without interrupting or judging. Be still and listen to learn.

2. **Express Gratitude and Appreciation:**

    Regularly express appreciation for the people in your life and the positive aspects of your relationships. Gratitude fosters feelings of connection and strengthens bonds.

3. **Share Vulnerability:**

   Be willing to share your own feelings and experiences authentically, allowing others to do the same. Vulnerability builds trust and deepens emotional connections. Be genuine, show up and trust yourself.

4. **Engage in Meaningful Conversations:**

   Have open and honest discussions about meaningful topics that matter to you and those around you. Share your thoughts, values, and aspirations to foster understanding and connection.

5. **Show Empathy and Compassion:**

   Practise empathy by putting yourself in others' shoes and understanding their perspectives and emotions. Show compassion and support to those who are going through difficult times.

6. **Create Rituals of Connection:**

   Establish regular rituals or traditions that bring people together, such as family dinners, game nights, or group outings. These shared experiences strengthen bonds and create lasting memories, but making them meaningful with a purpose, not a traditional tick box. This requires true heart!

7. **Celebrate Milestones and Achievements:**

   Acknowledge and celebrate the accomplishments and milestones of your loved ones. Celebrating together fosters a sense of belonging and reinforces positive connections. Don't let your money trauma stories stunt your generosity to celebrate — don't sabotage!

8. **Offer Support and Encouragement:**

   Be there for others in times of need, offering support, encouragement, and practical assistance when necessary. Acts of kindness and support strengthen relationships and build trust. Practise this intentionally with family and as often as possible — with friends it comes too easily!

9. **Practise Forgiveness:**

   Let go of past grievances and practise forgiveness towards yourself and others. Forgiveness frees up emotional energy and allows for deeper connections to flourish. Practice makes perfect!

10. **Prioritise Quality Time:**

    Make time for meaningful interactions with loved ones, free from distractions and interruptions. Quality time allows for deeper connection and strengthens emotional bonds. Even when it is scary, do it — it's worth it!

Nurture your own HEART and cultivate meaningful emotional connections daily with others. Notice the difference in your life — notice being a Wahine Warrior!

A Wahine Warrior Embraces WISDOM

One day, I came home to find my husband still there when he should have been at work. As I pulled up in the car, he came out to greet me, saying, 'I really need to talk to you.' Those words scared me because it was out of character for him, and my mind raced to all the worst possibilities — was it adultery or some other immoral practice? He took my hand, asked me to sit down, and explained that while vacuuming under our bed, he had come across my journals. He admitted he never intended to pry, but as he restacked them, one fell open, and he began to read it. He couldn't put it down. He lovingly hugged me, sharing that he had no idea what I had been through. Reading my journal and feeling my pain was why he couldn't go to work. He wanted to be with me, to hold me, protect me, comfort me, and love me. In that moment, I realised that true love and understanding come from a wise heart, capable of empathising with another's journey without judgment or fear.

Wise hearts with wisdom was a notable strength among my trauma Wahine Warrior group also. Each of us recognised that we were still a work-in-progress, striving to evolve into the best versions of ourselves. We understood that healing and education were intertwined, comprehending that our brains had the capacity to develop new neurotransmitters, enabling us to catalyse change. Our determination to avoid repeating past mistakes stemmed from our desire for improved futures for ourselves, our children, and generations to come. We embraced a forward-looking vision, understanding that, without it, our families would falter. With this mindset, we eagerly exchanged our successes and shared pearls of wisdom.

Here are some strategies for seeking wisdom:

1. **Be Curious:**

    Cultivate a curious mindset and a thirst for knowledge. Ask questions, explore new ideas, and seek out diverse perspectives to broaden your understanding of the world.

2. **Read Widely:**

    Make reading a habit and explore a variety of topics,

genres, and authors. Books, articles, and essays are treasure troves of wisdom and insights waiting to be discovered.

3. **Seek Mentorship:**

   Surround yourself with wise and experienced individuals who can offer guidance, support, and valuable life lessons. Learn from their experiences and seek their advice when faced with challenges.

4. **Reflect Regularly:**

   Set aside time for self-reflection and introspection. Reflecting on your experiences, actions, and decisions can provide valuable insights into your strengths, weaknesses, and areas for growth.

5. **Practise Mindfulness:**

   Cultivate mindfulness through practices such as meditation, deep breathing, and mindfulness exercises. Being present in the moment can help you gain clarity, focus, and a deeper understanding of yourself and the world around you.

6. **Embrace Failure and Mistakes:**

   View failure and mistakes as opportunities for learning and growth rather than setbacks. Embrace them with humility, curiosity, and a willingness to learn from your experiences.

7. **Engage in Meaningful Conversations:**

   Seek out meaningful conversations with friends, family members, colleagues, and mentors. Engage in deep discussions on topics that matter to you and be open to listening and learning from others.

8. **Stay Humble:**

   Recognise that wisdom is a lifelong journey, and no one has all the answers. Stay humble and open-minded, acknowledging that there is always more to learn and discover.

9. **Practice Empathy and Compassion:**

   Cultivate empathy and compassion towards yourself and others. Seek to understand the perspectives and experiences of those around you, and approach interactions with kindness, empathy, and respect.

10. **Stay Curious:**

    Never stop learning and seeking knowledge. Keep an open mind, stay curious, and remain receptive to new ideas, perspectives, and experiences.

Embark on a journey of seeking wisdom and continue to grow and evolve as a person — you will love falling in love with being a Wahine Warrior!

Echoing the beautiful Tongan proverb at the beginning of this chapter, *'Fakakaukau ke tauhi e 'ofa, ke tauhi e loto, mo e maama'a,'* which translates to, *'Be prepared to embrace love, embrace the heart, and embrace wisdom.'* It emphasises the importance of readiness to accept love, nurture the heart and seek wisdom.

A
WAHINE WARRIOR
embraces LOVE,
nurtures the HEART,
always with WISDOM.

She has these attributes to
navigate challenges
and find resilience
in the face of adversity.

*'Fa'amaliega i ōu tupuna, ona mafai ai e
fesoasoani iā te oe i taimi e uiga iā te oe.'*
'Trust in your ancestors, for they will aid you when needed.'

Chapter 8:
Beyond the veil

During my final year as a master's student in psychotherapy, my university organised a 'noho marae' experience. The motivation behind this cultural immersion within a Eurocentric education system was rooted in biculturalism to honour the principles of 'te tiriti', *Treaty of Waitangi*. However, as someone familiar with Tikanga Māori, I found that the protocols observed on the marae, a communal and sacred space, did not align with my understanding of Māori customs.

Intuitively, I sensed this misalignment within my indigenous identity. We were participating in a group training session at the university marae, seated in chairs arranged in a circle. This setting felt profoundly awkward and uncomfortable for me, because we were practicing a pakeha Eurocentric practicum in a Māori setting. Usually, this weekly group session took place on campus in a classroom and the tutors didn't appear to respect the kaupapa, *the foundational principles*, of being on marae.

In a moment driven by my Wahine Warrior spirit, I took action. Without uttering a word, I replaced my chair with a mattress and seated myself upon it. All eyes turned toward me, but I remained silent initially. Eventually, I spoke up, expressing that in this sacred space of the marae, I would adhere to 'Tikanga Māori'. I emphasised that it is the marae, with its carvings, symbolism, and ancestral presence, that guides our proceedings, not the tutors. Sitting on the mattress exemplified my respect and values for Tikanga Māori and my belief in the realm that exists beyond the veil. Up until that moment in my life, I wasn't even aware of what I intrinsically, or spiritually, have always known and believed. It was truly a magnificent moment that lit my spirit on fire!

I didn't seek permission; I felt an inherent 'right' and determination to act. The concept of 'tino rangatiratanga', *self-determination*, resonated strongly. I felt the comforting presence of my great-grandmother, Peleise, enveloping me. Though I rarely have experiences with departed loved ones, I did so at a time of doubt during my master's studies. I was ready to give up, I was done! But my grandma Peleise visited me. I'd never had an experience like this, and now knew that the veil between this life and the next was close.

I felt so special that SHE emerged from beyond the veil for ME! I felt her visit with me, her encouragement and warmth, urging me to persevere. It was an experience I could not deny, and I know that I come from a noble line of Wahine Warriors. As a grandmother I resonate strongly, because when I pass away, I would come and visit my great-grandchildren when they desperately need comfort, peace, and love.

I intend to ask my grandma Peleise: *why did she forbid Samoan language being spoken at home?* My maternal grandfather, of Chinese-Samoan descent, bore a Chinese surname, and discrimination against us was inescapable. Grandma Peleise's decision to prioritise English in their household, while understandable, left me feeling disconnected and insufficiently Samoan. The intergenerational belief that English was superior only perpetuated this narrative, which proved to be unfulfilling. Maybe that is why she visited me on that day, when I felt so culturally conflicted. It feels like she knew I would find my way back to my cultural roots.

On that day, within the marae, as I stood embodying the strength of a Wahine Warrior, Grandma Peleise's spirit stood beside me. I take pride in my lineage of Wahine Warriors, both those who walk among us and those who have departed. With that experience in mind, I'm writing this book to call upon our Wahine Warrior ancestors across the Pacific to be with each reader, to comfort them, to encourage them, to see them, to value them, to love them.

In the Bible, there is a verse by the prophet Malachi: *'The hearts of the children shall turn to their fathers.'* To turn to our ancestors with a remembrance of our strengths, the wars, the great sacrifices, and especially the love for our people. Our determination to raise strong faithful, kind, loving families — unlike the movie, *Once Were Warriors*, that depicted us as abusive and cruel, ugly human beings. We are not that! We were, and still are, and will always be Wahine Warriors!

Wahine Warrior

With genuine gratitude and heartfelt appreciation, this dedication is to the Wahine Warriors of generations past.

Kia Kaha Te Rongo Pai

Ka ora, ka ora, ka ora!
We live, we live, we live!
Ka titiro ki te rangi!
Look to the sky!
Ka titiro ki te whenua!
Look to the land!
Ka tangi te manu, ka tangi te kāhu!
The birds cry, the hawk cries!
Kia kaha, kia kaha, kia kaha!
Be strong, be strong, be strong!
Kia Kaha Te Rongo Pai!
May peace be strong!

Wahine Warriors of the past,
Their strength and power ever last.
Through storms they sailed, with hearts so bold,
Guided by ancestors, wise and old.

Their sacrifices, their love profound,
In their footsteps, our path is found.
With faith in God, who guides the sea,
We navigate life, strong and free.

With strength and power, we embrace
Our heritage, our sacred place.
United we stand, in love and light,
With ancestors' blessings, shining bright.

In their memory, we stand tall,
Their spirit within us, we heed their call.
For always were, and still are we,
Wahine Warriors we shall be!

Ka ora, ka ora, ka ora!
We live, we live, we live!
Ka titiro ki te rangi!
Look to the sky!
Ka titiro ki te whenua!
Look to the land!
Kia kaha, kia kaha, kia kaha!
Be strong, be strong, be strong!
Kia Kaha Te Rongo Pai!
May peace be strong!

In Your Ancestry: Find Your Wahine Warrior

1. **Embrace Strength and Resilience:**

   Recognise the strength and resilience inherent in your ancestry. Our Wahine Warrior ancestors faced challenges head-on, demonstrating unwavering determination and courage in the face of adversity.

2. **Learn from Sacrifices and Wisdom:**

   Reflect on the sacrifices made by our ancestors and the wisdom they imparted. Their experiences teach us valuable lessons about perseverance, selflessness, and the importance of community.

3. **Celebrate Cultural Heritage:**

   Embrace and celebrate our cultural heritage and traditions. Our Wahine Warrior ancestors passed down rich cultural practices that instil pride and a sense of belonging in us today.

4. **Nurture Family Bonds:**

   Cherish and nurture family bonds, just as our ancestors did. Their love and support for one another served as the foundation for building strong, resilient families and communities.

5. **Empower Through Identity:**

   Find empowerment in your ancestral identity. Our Wahine Warrior ancestors blazed trails, challenging societal norms, and paving the way for future generations to embrace their heritage with pride.

6. **Follow Role Models for Change:**

   Look to our Wahine Warrior ancestors as role models for positive change. Their actions and leadership inspire us to make a difference in our communities and strive for a better future.

7. **Keep the Stories Alive:**

   Preserve and share ancestral stories to keep our heritage alive. As Wahine Warriors, we have a responsibility to pass down these stories to future generations, ensuring that our legacy continues to inspire and empower.

Below in italics is a recent personal journal entry in March 2024, sharing about my Siva Samoa dance classes:

Every class, especially the first, I felt emotional, crying inside. I've felt the same in every session in lesser degrees, and there's a part of me that just wants to SIVA with all my soul, but for fear of looking so dumb and awkward, I stay very reserved... I always love watching the children, as they are so free, liberated with no inhibitions and as I watch the youth, so confident, happy, joyful, embracing it all creatively with indigenous joy, I am so touched, and I wish when I was growing up, I had a 'Matavai' village in my life — how that would have made a difference. I think this is my grief, even pain of feeling cut off from who I am inside, cut off from my ancestors denying myself of the richness of legacy that you manifest.

I love watching my moko (grandchild) belong and embrace all parts of their cultural heritage and heal from them too. God bless them always; I am ever so grateful...

I am 62 years old, and it is never too late. Learning to Siva Samoa — dance Samoan — has helped me embrace my identity and heal. I imagine my entry to meet my ancestors will be a joyous occasion with song and dance and, to know them, is to love them. I invite you to take a moment to honour the legacy of your ancestral Wahine Warrior. Although, I refer to my ancestral wahine warriors as females, they might also be males — alas they are all heroes that nurture us from the other side of the veil. Here are some suggestions for ways you can honour them and connect with your ancestral roots:

1. **Write in Your Journal:**

   Set aside some time to write in your journal about your ancestral Wahine Warrior. Reflect on her qualities, her triumphs, and the challenges she faced. Consider how her strength and resilience continue to inspire you today. Writing down your thoughts and feelings can be a powerful way to honour her legacy and deepen your connection to your ancestry.

2. **Visit a Relative:**

   Reach out to a relative who may have stories or memories of your ancestral Wahine Warrior. Spend time with them, listening to their recollections and learning more about your family history. Connecting with living relatives can provide valuable insights into your ancestral heritage and help you better understand the impact of your Wahine Warrior's legacy.

3. **Visit a Gravesite:**

   If possible, visit the gravesite of your ancestral Wahine Warrior. Take a moment to pay your respects, offer gratitude, and reflect on her life and legacy. You may choose to bring flowers or other tokens of remembrance as a tribute to her memory. Spending time at her gravesite can be a deeply meaningful way to honour her and feel connected to your ancestry.

4. **Spend Time Remembering:**

   Set aside dedicated time to remember your ancestral Wahine Warrior in your own way. Light a candle, say a prayer, or simply sit in quiet contemplation, allowing her spirit to guide and inspire you. Reflect on the lessons she taught through her actions and the values she upheld. By spending time remembering her, you honour her legacy and keep her spirit alive in your heart.

Whatever you choose to do, remember that honouring your ancestral Wahine Warrior is a deeply personal and meaningful journey. Embrace the opportunity to connect with your roots, celebrate her legacy, and draw strength from her enduring spirit. As you reflect on her life and legacy, may you find inspiration and guidance for your own journey as a Wahine Warrior in today's world. 'Fa'amaliega i ōu tupuna, ona mafai ai e fesoasoani iā te oe i taimi e uiga iā te oe.' *This Samoan quote to* 'Trust in your ancestors, for they will aid you when needed' *has been a priceless deep spiritual connection from beyond the veil.*

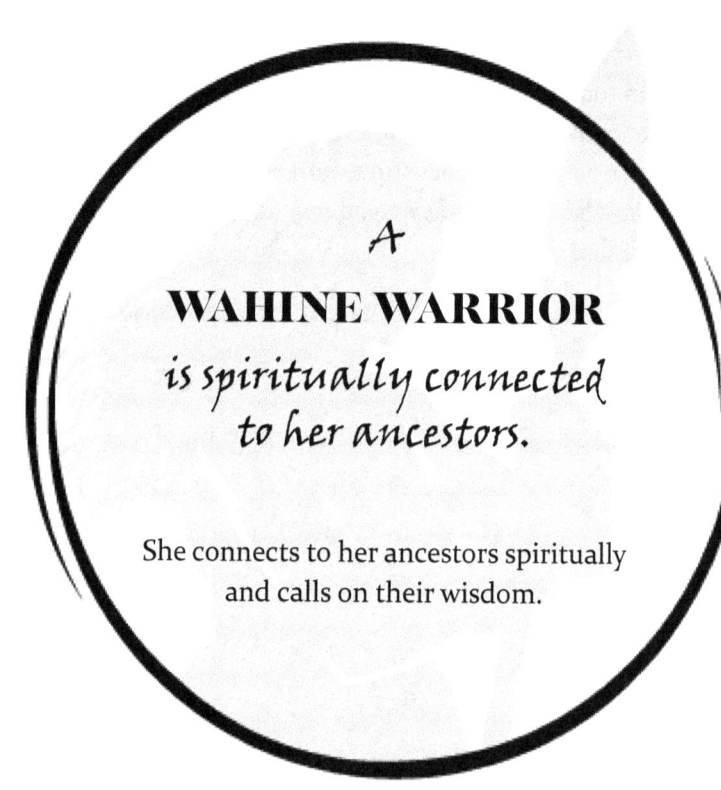

A
WAHINE WARRIOR
is spiritually connected to her ancestors.

She connects to her ancestors spiritually
and calls on their wisdom.

Definitions:

Kaupapa

'Kaupapa' is a Māori term that can be translated to mean *purpose, principle, policy,* or *agenda*. It encompasses the foundational ideas, goals, values, and plans that guide an individual, group, organisation, or community in their actions, decisions, and initiatives.

In a broader sense, 'kaupapa' can also refer to the overarching framework or philosophy that underpins a particular movement, project, or program. For example, in the context of academic research or community development, a kaupapa-driven approach emphasises the importance of centering indigenous perspectives, values, and priorities.

'Kaupapa Māori' specifically refers to a Māori-centred approach or framework that prioritises Māori perspectives, knowledge, and aspirations. It emphasises the empowerment and well-being of Māori individuals and communities and is often used in various fields, including education, health, politics, and social services, to address issues and challenges facing Māori people in Aotearoa, *New Zealand*.

Noho Marae

In Māori culture, a marae is a communal or sacred place that serves various social, cultural, and spiritual purposes for the community. It often includes a wharenui, *meeting house,* and other buildings where gatherings, ceremonies, and other important events take place. 'Noho' generally means to *stay* or *reside*, so 'noho marae' refers to *staying* or *residing at the marae for a period*, often for cultural events, ceremonies, or gatherings.

Tino rangatiratanga

'Tino Rangatiratanga' represents the inherent right of Māori to govern themselves, make decisions about their own affairs, and control their resources. It embodies the idea of self-determination and autonomy for Māori as the indigenous people of New Zealand.

The concept gained prominence during the Māori renaissance in the late 20th century, as Māori communities and activists sought to assert their rights and push for greater recognition of their cultural and political aspirations. 'Tino Rangatiratanga' has been a central principle in negotiations between the New Zealand government and Māori iwi, *tribes*, regarding issues such as treaty settlements, resource management, and constitutional reform.

In 1840 the Treaty of Waitangi, signed between representatives of the British Crown and Māori chiefs, recognised Māori as the tangata whenua, *people of the land*, and guaranteed them certain rights and protections. While interpretations of the treaty have varied over time, 'Tino Rangatiratanga' represents Māori efforts to uphold their treaty rights and assert their sovereignty within the framework of a modern New Zealand society.

Tikanga Māori

'Tikanga Māori' refers to the customs, protocols, values, and practices of the Māori people, the indigenous Polynesian people of New Zealand. It encompasses traditional Māori ways of doing things, including social interactions, ceremonies, rituals, language usage, and relationships with the natural world. 'Tikanga Māori' is deeply rooted in Māori culture and worldview and guides behaviour, decision-making, and relationships within Māori communities.

Key aspects of 'tikanga Māori' include concepts such as 'mana', *prestige, authority, power*; 'whakapapa', *genealogy, interconnectedness*; 'kaitiakitanga', *guardianship of the environment*; and 'whanaungatanga', *relationships and kinship*. 'Tikanga Māori' is considered integral to the identity and well-being of Māori individuals and communities, and efforts to revitalise and preserve 'tikanga Māori' are ongoing in New Zealand.

Whakapapa

'Whakapapa' is a Māori term that encompasses the concept of *genealogy, lineage,* and *interconnectedness*. It refers to the genealogical links that connect Māori individuals and communities to their ancestors, as well as to the natural world.

'Whakapapa' is more than just a family tree; it is a complex and dynamic system of relationships that trace ancestral lines through generations, connecting people to their past, present, and future. It encompasses not only biological ancestry but also spiritual and cultural connections.

In Māori culture, 'whakapapa' is deeply respected and plays a central role in identity, belonging, and understanding one's place in the world. It informs social structure, relationships, and obligations within Māori communities. 'Whakapapa' is often shared through oral tradition, storytelling, and ceremonial practices, preserving ancestral knowledge and wisdom for future generations.

'Whakapapa' also extends beyond human lineage to include connections to the land, animals, plants, and elements of nature. This holistic understanding of 'whakapapa' emphasises the interconnectedness and interdependence of all living beings and highlights the importance of stewardship and respect for the natural world.

Overall, 'whakapapa' is a fundamental concept in Māori culture that reflects the rich tapestry of relationships that bind individuals, families, communities, and the environment together. It serves as a foundation for Māori identity, culture, and values.

*'Ngurra ngurra balan bama ngandji,
yanha balan wargunu.'*
'Step by step, we heal, and together we grow.'

Chapter 9: I forgive you, please forgive me

In May 2015, as I was getting ready to depart from New Zealand following a memorable family occasion, I made my usual visit to our family home to say goodbye to my mother. It had become a tradition for me before heading to the airport. Nevertheless, even after bidding farewell, I felt the urge to dial her number once more from my mobile while on the way to the airport. It struck me as unusual to say goodbye twice, but in that moment, I felt a profound peace wash over me. I realised that I had come to terms with the complexities of our mother-daughter relationship. Despite its imperfections, I accepted it as the best that it could be.

In February 2024, while I was abroad, a close friend contacted me. Aware of her spiritual gifts, I courageously inquired if she had dreamt about me. Confirming my hunch, she delicately probed to check on my well-being, as her dream depicted me in profound sorrow, mourning someone. I shared that my brother had recently passed away, expressing appreciation for her care and her remarkable gifts.

When we met in person, we explored the depths of her dream further. As we unravelled its meaning together, I was moved to realise that beneath the surface lay a profound longing for forgiveness from my mother, a need I had believed I had already resolved. A particularly striking moment was when my gifted friend requested a photo and identified my mother's presence in the dream — a powerful acknowledgment of her desire for reconciliation from beyond the veil. This resonated deeply with me, and I felt that my younger brother was with her, perhaps sharing some of my earthly challenges with our mother.

While such experiences may not be common to everyone, as a Pacific Islander woman and a believer in spiritual connections, this moment struck a chord with me. It reminded me of a previous encounter I had with my deceased great-grandmother, reinforcing my belief in the profound connections and meaningful messages that can transcend the physical realm. I am thinking this book is really to help me understand my mother, what happened to her, and the need for me to truly forgive her.

Throughout my upbringing, my mother's actions and attitudes often seemed to mirror unresolved wounds from her past. There were periods when we were close, but I often felt overwhelmed. Our relationship sometimes felt co-dependent, which wasn't healthy; I would often distance myself to maintain some breathing space.

As I immerse myself in the journey of forgiving my mother, memories of past experiences have stirred up deep-seated pain and turmoil within me. Despite these challenging emotions, I find immense value in the process. It's like the ache of muscles after pushing oneself to lift heavier weights—the discomfort is a necessary part of growth, a sign that we're expanding our capacity. Similarly, forgiving and healing involves nurturing new pathways in our minds and hearts, akin to fostering resilience and understanding. Integrating neuroscience with the profound healing journey helps me honour both the emotional and physiological aspects of transformation and recovery.

This has been one of the most challenging and deeply personal journeys I have undertaken, and even now there are steps I need to consider as I navigate the path toward full forgiveness:

1. **Acknowledge My Pain:**

    Recognise and validate my own feelings of hurt, anger, and betrayal. It's essential to acknowledge the impact my mother's actions and words have had on me before I can begin the process of forgiveness.

    This book I am writing has become a powerful tool in this process, allowing me to confront my pain, validate my emotions, and strive to understand my mother's actions. The feelings I am experiencing may be ones I have suppressed and tried to keep hidden, but now that I am allowing myself to acknowledge them, I feel a sense of liberation. I am no longer bound by these suppressed emotions and can embrace the freedom to be still, to be myself, and to know that I am enough. I recognise that I am a Wahine Warrior, strong and capable of navigating through this journey of healing and forgiveness.

2. **Understand Her Perspective:**

   Try to gain insight into my mother's experiences and the factors that may have contributed to her behaviour. Consider her upbringing, life experiences, and any unresolved trauma she may have carried from her own past.

   Although my mother didn't share much about her life, I now realise that perhaps I wasn't curious enough or didn't ask enough questions. However, I do recall certain details, such as her own journey of leaving home. Life in the islands can be challenging, and my mother's transition to New Zealand with her father, preceding her mother, suggests a complex family dynamic.

   As a teenager, she was thrust into adulthood, forced to work and forfeit her education — a heavy responsibility that undoubtedly cut her childhood short. These experiences likely shaped her perspectives, values, and approach to life, offering valuable insight into understanding her behaviour and actions.

3. **Practise Empathy:**

   Cultivate empathy by putting yourself in your mother's shoes and imagining what she may have been feeling or experiencing at the time. Recognise that her actions may have been influenced by her own pain and struggles.

   My relationship with my maternal grandmother was strained; I never seemed to rank high on her list of favourite grandchildren, always lingering far down the pecking order. It was evident that my mother, too, faced her own challenges in her relationship with her mother. While she shared a close bond with her father, her connection with her mother seemed distant.

The rift deepened when my mother's parents deceived my father. He had paid them money, believing he was purchasing their property. Instead, they absconded with the funds and went on a mission. This betrayal not only burned bridges but also inflicted pain and heartache on my parents' marriage.

4. **Set Boundaries:**

    Establish clear boundaries to protect yourself from further harm while still allowing space for healing and reconciliation. Boundaries can help you maintain your emotional well-being as you navigate your relationship with your mother.

    Identifying triggers and being aware of my feelings is a great first step. My experience of feeling torn between my triggers — being annoyed and then resentful — were always at play. I found that setting boundaries with a clear purpose is essential. Understanding why I need these boundaries can help me communicate them effectively and stay committed to them, even in the face of pushback — whether it's to protect my mental health, prioritise my own well-being, or establish healthier dynamics in our relationship. Having a clear understanding of my 'why' provided the strength and conviction needed to uphold my boundaries.

    Setting boundaries was not about punishing or rejecting my mother; it was about creating a healthier dynamic where both parties can thrive. Communicating your boundaries calmly and assertively, while also being open to dialogue and compromise, can help facilitate understanding and potentially lead to healing and reconciliation in the long run.

5. **Release Resentment:**

    Holding onto resentment only prolongs your pain and prevents you from moving forward. Practise letting go of bitterness and resentment by acknowledging the hurt but choosing not to dwell on it or let it consume you.

    I've harboured many resentments towards my mother. Letting go requires you to search your soul and be honest with yourself. Obesity was something my mother and I shared. For many years she and I were morbidly obese. I recall my mother being rushed to hospital in absolute agony with a severe attack of gallstones. As the attending physician examined her, he was overwhelmed not knowing where the stomach began or ended.

    The doctor politely asked her what she ate, and she promptly replied, 'Oh, I hardly eat anything!' He then turned to me for a more realistic honest answer. Denial is often used when we are not ready to change. Being honest and ready to change is required to release resentment. In fact, releasing resentment is like losing weight. It's not something you do once and forget about. Here's why:

    5.1 **It Takes Time:**

    Just like losing weight takes time, letting go of resentment is a gradual process.

    5.2 **Keep Working at It:**

    You need to keep working at releasing resentment, just like you keep working at losing weight by eating healthy and exercising regularly.

5.3 **There Will Be Ups and Downs:**

Like weight loss, you'll have good days and bad days. Sometimes you'll feel better, and sometimes old feelings will come back.

5.4 **Stay Consistent:**

Releasing resentment requires consistent effort, like sticking to a healthy routine for weight loss.

5.5 **It's a Lifestyle Change:**

Letting go of resentment isn't just about one incident — it's about changing how you think and feel in the long term, just like maintaining weight loss is about changing your lifestyle.

5.6 **Change Your Mindset:**

You must change the way you think about things, like forgiving instead of holding onto grudges.

Overall, releasing resentment is a gradual and iterative process that requires patience, self-awareness, and ongoing effort. It involves not only addressing past grievances but also cultivating resilience, compassion, and a sense of inner peace.

6. **Cultivate Compassion:**

Foster a sense of compassion toward your mother, recognising her humanity and inherent worth despite her flaws and mistakes. Understand that forgiveness is an act of compassion, both for yourself and for her.

Extending compassion to my mother proved challenging, given my lack of trust in her. My traumatised inner child often dominated, keeping me in a constant state of protection. Yet, I found solace in her strong work ethic and dedication to serving others — traits I've inherited and deeply value. Breathing in her spirit of service, I realise it's become intrinsic to my being — I know no other way of life because of her teachings. My gratitude transforms into compassion, which in turn fosters forgiveness. Thank you, Mum!

7. **Focus on Healing:**

   Prioritise your own healing and well-being as you work through the forgiveness process. Engage in self-care practices that nurture your physical, emotional, and spiritual health.

   My mother was somewhat of a martyr, so she didn't prioritise her own healing and well-being. We often refer to that generation as 'old school' where you can't teach old dogs new tricks. Self-care and burn-out would be seen as selfish and weak. I hope that we are not 'old school' and will embrace self-care as preventative and proactive and deserving! Committing to healing requires significant effort that cannot be underestimated.

   Prioritising our health, particularly our mental well-being, allows us to honour our body, mind, and soul, and directs our attention towards overall well-being. In today's fast-paced, constantly evolving world, it's easy to become distracted and engulfed in busyness, neglecting opportunities to pause, be still, and fully immerse ourselves in the present moment. Taking time to appreciate the beauty around us, to breathe deeply, and to cultivate gratitude for the abundance in our lives is essential for genuine living.

8. **Seek Support:**

    Consider seeking support from a therapist, counsellor, life coach, or support group who can provide guidance, validation, and perspective as you navigate the complexities of forgiveness.

    I had a particular hard day at work. I was a social worker with Barnardo's and the child abuse that day was horrific. In the car with my mother, I shared my feelings of feeling sickened at what adults can do to children. My mother's advice was: 'Oh, you'll get used to it,' which I also interpreted as: 'Harden up!' She was a volunteer in a women's refuge with little therapeutic skills and I was embarking on my career in social work. I silently thought that I would always want to vomit and feel sick with child abuse cases, I didn't want to be desensitised and normalise it.

    Seeking support is paramount! Don't try to be a hero or a martyr. Stay true to yourself in your convictions. Your feelings are real, and they are often your superpower! But don't be too proud to seek quality support — even therapy or counselling to be grounded, be real and be the best you can be!

9. **Practise Forgiveness:**

    Forgiveness is a process, not a one-time event. It may involve multiple stages and revisiting the decision to forgive as you continue to heal and grow. Practise forgiveness as an ongoing journey of releasing resentment and embracing compassion.

    'Practise Forgiveness' — that sounds so cheesy! Well, let's think about that. We all know that if we want to be good

at something, like sport, dancing, performing arts etc, we must practice, practice, practice! So, think of it this way:

9.1 **Repetition and Effort:**

Like practising a musical instrument, forgiving someone takes time and repeated effort. It's something you work on consistently to get better at it.

9.2 **Learning from Mistakes:**

Just as you learn from mistakes when playing music, forgiveness involves learning from past hurts and moving forward without dwelling on them.

9.3 **Being Patient:**

Both learning an instrument and forgiving someone require patience. You won't see immediate results, but progress comes with time and practice.

9.4 **Getting Stronger:**

Practising an instrument builds resilience and forgiving others can make you emotionally stronger by helping you bounce back from tough situations.

9.5 **Expressing Yourself:**

Playing music lets you express your emotions, and forgiving others allows you to express your feelings in a healthy way, leading to healing.

9.6 **Finding Balance:**

Like creating harmony in music, forgiveness brings balance to your life and relationships. It's about finding peace and understanding in difficult situations.

9.7 **Connecting with Others:**
Playing music with others creates a connection, just like forgiving someone can strengthen your relationships and bring you closer to others.

*Above is why we need to practise.
Below is what we need to do —
it is in the doing that we truly learn:*

9.8 **Acknowledge Your Feelings:**
Start by recognising and accepting how you feel — whether it's hurt, anger, or resentment. It's important to understand your emotions before you can forgive.

9.9 **Understand the Situation:**
Try to see things from the other person's perspective. This doesn't mean you're okay with what happened, but understanding why it happened can help you move forward.

9.10 **Let Go of Negative Feelings:**
Decide to release negative emotions like anger and resentment. Holding onto them only hurts you in the long run.

9.11 **Show Empathy and Compassion:**
Be kind to yourself and the person who hurt you. Everyone makes mistakes, and showing understanding can help you heal.

9.12 **Set Boundaries:**

Protect yourself from further harm by setting healthy boundaries. This might mean limiting contact with the person who hurt you or being clear about what you expect from them in the future.

9.13 **Take Care of Yourself:**

Make sure to look after yourself physically and emotionally. Doing things you enjoy and prioritising your well-being can help you through the forgiveness process.

9.14 **Get Support:**

Talk to people you trust — friends, family, or a therapist — about how you're feeling. They can offer advice and support as you work through your emotions.

9.15 **Let Go of Resentment:**

Forgiveness is about freeing yourself from resentment. It takes time, but by being patient and persistent, you can find peace and healing.

Remember, forgiveness isn't about forgetting what happened or saying it's okay — it's about finding peace within yourself and moving forward.

1. **Release Expectations:** Let go of expectations of how your mother should respond or behave. Forgiveness is ultimately about freeing yourself from the burden of resentment, regardless of how your mother chooses to respond.

My mother passed away 7 years ago and in writing this book, I didn't know I needed to forgive her. I had mistaken my 'acceptance' of our relationship as 'forgiveness'.

I see her love for me more clearly and remember these moments:

1. I had asked her to machine-hem my daughter's skirt for a formal she was attending at high school. The hemline was above the knee contrary to my mother's standard. My mother started lecturing me on how I shouldn't allow my teenager to dress immodestly. In her condescending manner she spoke in Samoan to my father to support her and my father intervened, speaking harshly to me to respect and honour my mother. I totally LOST it! I raised my voice to my father, and provocatively shouted, 'So, now you're going to be a father, and play that card? After everything you have put us through as children, you now want to try and play mum and dad now — HOW DARE YOU!!!' I stormed off in a fit of rage, so angry. My mother and father were gob-smacked and said nothing. An hour later my mother knocked at my front door with the clothing item altered to my request. Verbally there was no sorry, but I felt her sorrow, her love, and her compassion. I don't believe I had ever chastised them for their poor parenting, and they knew what I said to them was an accurate and true account. They saw my pain and held no resentment towards me.

2. At the passing of my father, the dynamics in the family home were too overwhelming for me. I didn't think anyone noticed, but I decided to slip away and returned to my home to be by myself. About an hour later, my mother turned up to my place and as

I opened the door, I sobbed, and she held me crying with me. A tender moment when I was seen, loved and validated. I am shedding tears as I recall this memory. Thank you, Mum x

---

Dear Mother, with love in my heart,
I write these words for a brand-new start.
Though shadows linger from days gone by,
I choose forgiveness, I'll let them fly.

For every tear shed and every pain,
I release them now, they're not in vain.
In the light of forgiveness,
I find my way
To heal the wounds of yesterday.

With empathy and compassion,
I embrace
The battles we've fought,
with poise and grace.
For in forgiving, I unleash my power,
A Wahine Warrior, in this very hour.

To love and be kind, I set us free
To write a new chapter, you and me.
So here's my hand, let's walk this road,
With more understanding,
we'll share the load.

Dear Mother, know this to be true:
I'm a Wahine Warrior, I forgive you.
But before we move forward,
there's something to say,
I ask for your forgiveness in every way.

For the times I faltered,
for the grief I have caused,
I seek your grace,
my mistakes I've paused.
Together, as warriors,
let's heal and grow,
With forgiveness as our strength,
our love will show.

I know my mother can read my poem from up above.

I love you, Mum, please forgive me x

17 April 2024

'Ngurra ngurra balan bama ngandji, yanha balan wargunu.' Translated, it means, 'Step by step, we heal, and together we grow.' I migrated to Australia 11 years ago and I am privileged to acknowledge the indigenous people of the land by using an Aboriginal proverb. This proverb reflects the journey of healing and growth of a Wahine Warrior.

'Ina soia, ma ia outou iloa o a'u lava o le Atua.'
Samoan

'Mou longo pe, pesa'ilo ko au koe 'Otua.'
Tongan

'Kia āta noho, ā kia mātau ko ahau te Atua.'
Maori

'Be still and know that I am God.'
Psalm 46:10

Chapter 10:
Be Still and Know that I AM

From my earliest memories as a child, escaping from the turmoil of domestic violence, I would pray fervently during each crisis, desperately pleading for the safety of my family. One memory stands out vividly: the day my mother and I returned home to news of yet another emergency. Before arriving to our house, our concerned neighbours rushed to meet us on the street, informing us of the situation and the visit of an ambulance. Sensing the gravity of the moment, my mother asked to use their restroom, bringing me along. In that small, confined space, my mother knelt and poured out her heart to God, pleading for the well-being and safety of her child.

Witnessing my mother's heartfelt prayer was a profound moment for me, especially since religious practices were not a part of our lives at the time. That day marked a significant turning point as my mother returned to her faith, and she brought us along with her on that spiritual journey. It was a transformative experience that affirmed the reality of God's presence and the power of prayer in our lives. Attending church offered me a variety of activities and programs. I discovered singing which became my refuge. The scriptures seemed complex and hard to grasp, yet music offered me a direct line to feeling the divine. Whether in choirs or alone, singing about God as my redeemer and Jesus Christ as my Saviour stirred deep emotions and spiritual connections within me.

My first personal revelation came when I was just 16 years old, attending boarding school. That particular year had been tumultuous, marked by emotional upheaval, trauma-informed behaviour, and the typical angst of adolescence. However, amidst this chaos, a turning point emerged. Midway through the year, my mother orchestrated a change of schools, a decision aimed at steering me back onto the path of righteous success.

As I settled into this new environment, my mindset shifted. Determined to overcome past struggles, I found a renewed sense of purpose, particularly as the crucial School Certificate exams loomed ahead. Despite a history of truancy and academic setbacks, I experienced a breakthrough during the practice exams. My results were actually good for someone who hadn't attended school much that year, but one subject was abysmal. In history, I achieved a mere 35 percent.

In the face of this challenge, my history teacher offered me a lifeline. He issued a challenge and a promise: if I committed to attending his tutorials diligently and put in the effort, he guaranteed that I would pass. This pledge became a beacon of hope, a tangible sign that with dedication and support, I could overcome obstacles and achieve academic success.

I made a pivotal decision to test my faith. In a heartfelt conversation with God, I dared to question His existence, despite the mistakes and slips that had marked my past. I pleaded for a chance to turn my life around, promising to strive for goodness and to clean up my act. With trembling sincerity, I begged for His intervention, even though I felt unworthy of His grace.

The heartfelt plea came to fruition during a national youth pageant held at the temple grounds, where a profound moment of divine revelation unfolded. I was participating as an actor in the pageant with hundreds of others. We had spent two weeks on-site during our school break, rehearsing scenes of warfare and a sacred visit from Christ. Reaching out to touch Christ was a deeply reverent and faith-strengthening experience. Despite the long hours and challenges, the mission to share this sacred message made the effort worthwhile. The spiritual bond among us was incredibly powerful.

As my peers eagerly received their envelopes containing their exam results, I held my breath, my heart heavy with anticipation. When my mother handed me my envelope, I hurried to a secluded spot to unveil its contents. I had performed admirably, but I was scanning for my history result — which was my answer to my prayer. In the subject I feared failing, I scored 50 percent. Against all odds, I had passed history and it felt like winning the lottery! My Heavenly Father had heard me, and I knew then that He was real, and He loved me.

In that sacred moment, the reality of God's presence washed over me like a flood of certainty. Overwhelmed with gratitude, I dropped to my knees, offering up a prayer of thanks. It wasn't just a passing grade; it was a divine affirmation — a perfect 50, demonstrating that His grace was all I needed. Years later, as I stood on the stage receiving honours for my master's degree, that 50 percent pass in history remained my highest academic achievement. It wasn't just a grade; it was a testament to the reality of God in my life. He knew me intimately, loved me unconditionally, and answered my prayer in a way that left no doubt of His existence.

Having God in my life brought me happiness, but it did not eliminate unhappy times. I had never known such profound loneliness until I became a single parent. I was struggling emotionally, praying for comfort and peace. This was the first Christmas season on my own, I felt utterly worthless and insignificant hitting rock bottom. Then, on Christmas Eve, there was a knock, and, on the doorstep, I found beautiful gifts left anonymously. Tears welled in my eyes as I realised that my prayers had been answered. In that moment, I felt an overwhelming sense of gratitude and love, knowing that God had heard me, that He knows me intimately, and that He loves me unconditionally. It was a powerful testament to the living reality of God in my life.

One particularly dark night, not long after separation in my first marriage, I found myself on the brink of despair. I had serious thoughts of ending my life and acted on them. Looking back, I can understand how I reached that harrowing place, yet I still carry a lingering sense of shame. I grappled with the notion that God allows trials to test and strengthen us, but I struggled to comprehend why He would allow me to entertain such dark thoughts. The experience of being rushed to the hospital, enduring the invasive procedure of having my stomach pumped, was a clear reminder of the depth of hopelessness I had reached. In that moment, I made a solemn vow, that I would never attempt to take my life again, no matter what.

It was a pivotal lesson — one that I believe God intended for me to learn. That promise became a lifeline, a beacon of hope in moments of darkness. Though I have found myself grappling with depressive states and suicidal thoughts since, I have held fast to that vow, knowing that breaking it would betray not only myself but also the trust I had placed in God.

Reflecting on that period, I am convinced that, had I not confronted those demons at that young age of 21, the outcome might have been far more tragic in later years. It is a testament to God's intimate knowledge of me, His guiding hand leading me through the darkest of valleys and reminding me of the promise that has kept me tethered to life. Amidst this journey, family has always been a crucial part of my support system.

I only knew my maternal grandparents. My siblings and I were their first grandchildren, and we shared a special bond at our Christmas gatherings. With all the extended families, especially our first cousins, aunties and uncles, these holiday reunions were always the highlight of the year.

On Christmas Eve, we would gather, anticipation hanging thick in the air as we waited for midnight. That's when 'data', our grandfather, would lead us in prayer — a prayer so long it seemed to stretch on for ages. Yet, even as young as I was, I felt something profound in those moments. There was a sense of safety, of boundless love, and an overwhelming peace that enveloped us all. Through the love and security of my extended family, was also how I came to know God.

My grandfather played a significant role in shaping my understanding of faith. He was always there to come to our rescue, providing a haven whenever we needed it most. His heartfelt prayers left an indelible mark on my heart, and every Christmas, I find myself pondering the reverence of his words of devotion. I am eternally grateful for the love and guidance he bestowed upon us. His prayers continue to echo in my heart, a reminder of the enduring presence of God in our lives, and the profound impact of love and family bonds.

Celebrating my 60th birthday during the covid lockdown was a unique challenge, but my children rose to the occasion with incredible creativity. They orchestrated a memorable celebration to mark this significant milestone in my life. As we brainstormed ideas for the theme of my birthday dinner, my youngest daughter posed a question that touched me deeply: 'So, Mum, besides Christmas and Jesus, what else do you love?'

Her words were the greatest compliment I had ever received. In that moment, my heart swelled with gratitude and love. It was a testament to the depth of her understanding and to the bond we shared. She knew me — she knew that my love for God and Jesus Christ was central to who I am.

*Through my unwavering faith
in Christ and His Atonement,
I have found true healing.
This faith is the foundation of my life,
the guiding force that sustains me
through every trial and triumph.
It is what I hold to be true above all else.*

For those who may not have a personal belief in God, the concept of being still and finding inner peace is valuable to heal from trauma. Here are some tips:

1. **Practise Mindfulness:**

    Take moments throughout your day to be still and present in the moment. Mindfulness techniques such as deep breathing, meditation, or focusing on your senses can help ground you and reduce feelings of anxiety or overwhelm.

2. **Seek Support:**

    Reach out to trusted friends, family members, or mental health professionals who can offer support and understanding as you navigate your healing journey. Talking about your experiences and feelings can be incredibly therapeutic.

3. **Engage in Self-Care:**

    Prioritise self-care activities that promote your physical, emotional, and mental well-being. This could include activities such as exercise, spending time in nature, creative expression, or enjoying hobbies that bring you joy.

4. **Educate Yourself:**

   Take time to learn about trauma and its effects on the mind and body. Understanding the impact of trauma can help you make sense of your experiences and identify healthy coping strategies.

5. **Set Boundaries:**

   Establish boundaries to protect your emotional and mental health. This may involve saying *no* to activities or situations that trigger distress or overwhelm and prioritising your own needs and well-being.

6. **Explore Healing Modalities:**

   Consider exploring different healing modalities such as therapy, support groups, art therapy, or holistic practices like yoga or acupuncture. Find what resonates with you and provides you with a sense of comfort and healing.

7. **Find Meaning and Purpose:**

   Reflect on your values, beliefs, and what gives your life meaning and purpose. Engage in activities that align with your values and help you feel connected to something greater than yourself, whether it's nature, community, or a sense of spirituality.

8. **Practice Gratitude:**

   Cultivate a practice of gratitude by focusing on the things in your life that you're thankful for, no matter how small. Gratitude can help shift your perspective and bring moments of joy and positivity amidst difficult times.

9. **Be Patient and Gentle with Yourself:**

    Healing from trauma takes time and patience. Be gentle with yourself as you navigate your journey and recognise that healing is a process with ups and downs. Celebrate your progress and acknowledge your resilience along the way.

By integrating these strategies into your daily life, you can foster inner peace and build resilience as you journey towards healing from trauma, even if you don't hold a personal belief in a higher power. My hope is for you to become a Wahine Warrior, empowered to overcome trauma and live a life free from its grip.

As I conclude my book, I feel privileged to share the timeless wisdom of *'Be still and know that I am God,'* found in Psalm 46:10. I offer it to you in my Samoan ancestral language: *'Fa'amanuia, ma mafaufau, o le Atua ou teu fa'aleleia.'* Additionally, I embrace my Tongan heritage to share in Tongan: *'Fakalahi, mo fakamalie, ka'u, ko ha 'eiki au.'* And to my beloved Aotearoa, the land of the long white cloud, where I was born and raised, the cherished island where my experiences unfolded: *'Whakarongo, kia mōhio koe, ko ahau te Atua.'* May you be still, discover the Wahine Warrior within, and truly know who you are!

A

WAHINE WARRIOR

values being still

and trusting God.

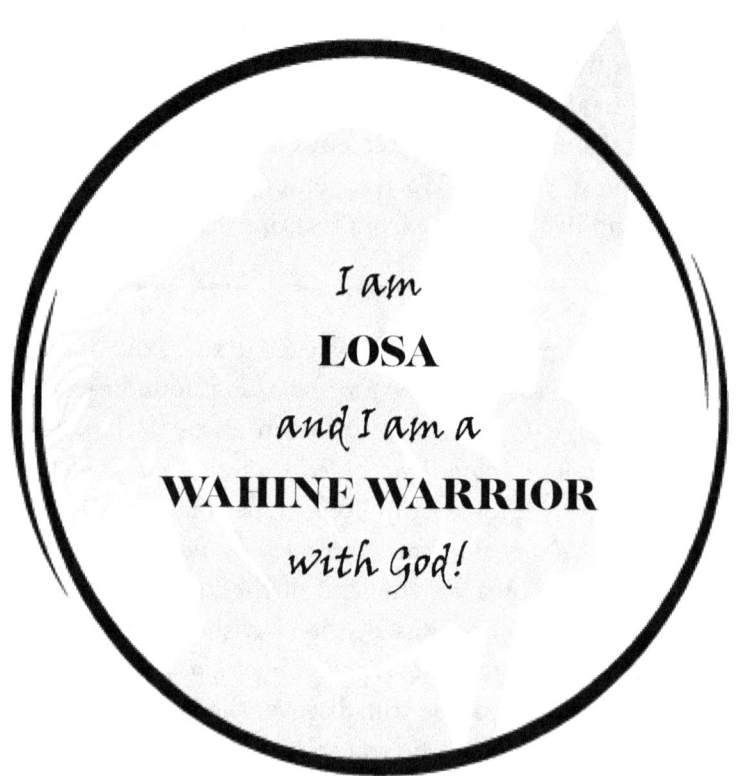

About the Author

Losa was born in 1961 in Auckland, New Zealand, embodies the spirit of lifelong learning and community dedication. Driven by her Samoan and Tongan heritage, she ventured back into academia as an adult, earning a master's degree in clinical psychotherapy in 2002. This pivotal achievement set the stage for her to become a beacon of mental health support within Pasifika communities.

Her career, a tapestry of diverse roles, ranges from grassroots support work to influential management positions in both government and non-government organisations. This broad spectrum of experience has armed Losa with a profound understanding of the intricacies and nuances of mental health care.

Losa's passion extends beyond individual care; she is a fervent advocate for developing a robust Pacific workforce. Through her commitment to capacity and leadership building, she empowers Pasifika people, ensuring they are equipped to uplift their communities.

Renowned as an inspiring trainer, clinical supervisor, and presenter, Losa is celebrated for her engaging storytelling and mana-enhancing approach. Her work transcends the boundaries of a mere career — it's a heartfelt calling. She finds great fulfillment in her role in transforming lives and changing the destinies of individuals and families for the better.

Outside of her professional life, Losa is a wife, mother, grandmother, sister, aunty, cousin and friend. She actively shares her insights and experiences across various platforms. Ever eager to connect, she thrives on engaging with others who share her fervour for mental health and community well-being. Her journey is a testament to the power of dedication, cultural pride, and the unyielding pursuit of making a difference.

She would LOVE to hear from you — here are her contact details:

- losapatterson@outlook.com
- https://losapatterson.com/
- https://www.facebook.com/losaskippspatterson
- https://www.facebook.com/groups/1013802555905980
- https://www.linkedin.com/in/losa-patterson-49816a171/

ENDORSEMENTS & TESTIMONIALS

With Love and Appreciation

In embarking on the journey of writing my first book — a deeply personal endeavour where I dared to bare my soul — I have been profoundly moved by the outpouring of generosity from those who have embraced its essence. As I invited people to give feedback on my manuscript, I was deeply honoured by the praise and accolades I received.

These endorsements and testimonies have strengthened me and wrapped me in the strength of our shared values and the unity of our Pacific community, resonating with the wisdom and resilience passed down through generations. This revered Māori proverb encapsulates the essence of our collective journey — a journey woven together by diverse voices, each contributing yarn to the sacred cloth of shared experiences.

> *'He aha te mea nui o te ao?*
> *He tangata, he tangata, he tangata.'*
> 'What is the most important thing in the world?
> It is people, it is people, it is people.'
>
> *Alofa tele, Losa Patterson*

Dr Shannon Said
Mental Health Clinician | Researcher and Academic

It takes an incredible amount of strength, determination and resilience to ask questions about the most foundational aspects of our lives, and those who raised us, in a quest to create new pathways and spiritual realities for those who come after us. In this brave and vulnerable book, this is exactly what Losa has done. Her commitment to the integrity of her *wairuatanga* and the wellbeing of her children, grandchildren, and future generations shines through in this book, sustained by empathy and deep appreciation for the wisdom of those who have gone before her. An insightful resource that I believe has the power to change generations!

Kara Watene-Zelezniak
Business Owner-Director | Counsellor

After reading Losa Patterson's book, 'Wahine Warrior,' I was left with a myriad of emotions, some familiar and others previously unexplored. There were numerous moments of overwhelming emotion, tears flowing as I journeyed through her narrative of self-healing, emphasizing the importance of love, kindness, understanding, forgiveness, and acceptance. This deeply resonated with me, highlighting the power of faith in a God who reminded her of her worth and unconditional love as His daughter.

I admire Losa's courage in penning this book and sharing personal experiences, allowing readers to connect with her journey of self-awareness and acceptance of her own worth. I appreciated how Losa provided steps and guidance on navigating challenging life experiences. Being of Māori descent, I found it touching when she included quotes in different languages to connect with our Polynesian heritage, fostering a deeper connection to becoming your own 'Wahine Warrior.'

Losa has crafted a powerful, inspiring, educational, and engaging book that I couldn't put down. One of my favourite parts was the poem she wrote to her mother, a beautiful tribute and testament to her healing journey. I wholeheartedly recommend this book to anyone grappling with trauma and seeking healing. It equips you with skills, strategies, and tools for your own healing journey.

Lesley Cyril
Family Focused Educator | Community Leader

Let *Wahine Warrior* change you. Losa's gifts as an author are evident as she relates deeply personal experiences in a relatable and vulnerable way. Her gifts as a life coach and counsellor shine as she clearly lays out how all women, but specifically Pasifika women, can turn trauma into powerful forgiveness and realised potential. I cannot recommend her book highly enough.

Diana Wong-Curuenavuli
CEO & Founder of Number 8 Prison Project | 2024 Zest Award Winner

Wahine Warrior is an evocative and compelling memoir that delves deep into Losa Patterson's life who, despite the challenges, rises above her circumstances to reclaim her strength and identity. This powerful narrative offers a raw and honest look at the struggles and triumphs of overcoming trauma.

Losa takes us so beautifully on an emotional journey, beginning with the painful experiences of her childhood. The portrayal of the events surrounding her parents is both heart-wrenching and poignant, capturing the profound impact such an environment can have on a child's psyche.

What sets *Wahine Warrior* apart is the Losa's unflinching honesty and resilience. Rather than succumbing to the weight of her trauma, she uses it as a catalyst for growth and transformation. Her journey from a place of pain to one of empowerment is both inspiring and uplifting. The memoir details her path to healing, illustrating how she confronted her past, sought support, and ultimately found ways to channel her experiences into a force for good.

The narrative of this book is infused with cultural richness, offering readers an intimate look at Samoan traditions and values. This cultural backdrop not only enriches the story but also underscores the importance of heritage in the author's journey to self-discovery and empowerment. Her reconnection with her roots becomes a vital part of her healing process, reinforcing the theme of cultural identity as a source of strength.

The writing in *Wahine Warrior* is vivid and evocative, bringing to life the emotional landscapes and the resilience of the human spirit. Losa's voice is authentic and compelling, making it easy for readers to connect with her story on a deeply personal level. Each chapter unfolds with a sense of raw truth and unwavering determination, making it impossible to put the book down.

In conclusion, *Wahine Warrior* is a testament to the indomitable spirit of a woman who refused to let her trauma define her. It is a story of courage, resilience, and the transformative power of embracing one's identity and experiences. This memoir is not just an account of overcoming adversity; it is a celebration of the strength that lies within us all. For anyone seeking inspiration or insight into the journey of healing from trauma, Wahine Warrior is an essential read. Congratulations, my sister, on this beautiful read.

Rauhena Chase
Real Estate Owner-Director | Trainer & Academic

Wahine Warrior, penned with heartfelt passion by Losa Patterson, moved me to tears, especially the poignant ode to her mother. Her writing, deeply soulful and authentic, made me feel honoured to join her on this emotional journey.

Melanie Fruean
OAM Order of Australia Medal | Chair NSW Council of Pacific Communities

This morning, I finished your book. I couldn't stop reading. Thank you for your bravery, rawness, and vulnerability. I found myself pausing to relate and reflect on my own journey several times. Losa, I have so much love and respect for you. The theme of 'kindness' resonates deeply and serves as a powerful reminder for us all. This book will be a beautiful gift to many, especially those like me who grapple with complex mother-daughter relationships and the generational struggles they entail. After reading, I realise I have healing to do with my daughters and my own mother.

At times, your truths were confronting, yet I appreciated the suggestions you offered after each chapter. The use of metaphors and Pacifica sayings enriched the reading experience. Thank you for writing this book; it serves as a poignant reminder that we can heal from intergenerational trauma. There's much more to digest, but for now, I will reflect on the profound impact of my morning readings. I leave you with this Whakataukī: 'Iti noa ana he pito mata. From the withered tree, a flower blooms.' This metaphor beautifully encapsulates your book's message — that even from what appears lifeless or strained, new life and beauty can emerge.

Arama Puriri
Area Pacific Manager | Accountant

Wahine Warrior captivated me to the point that I could not put the book down until I finished it. Losa's book drew me into each page with the same force as gravity, keeping me grounded in her narrative. Her vulnerability in sharing traumatic experiences felt all too familiar, painting vivid images in my mind, as if I were present. Each chapter ends with well-put-together, simplified steps and tips as a valuable resource. The respect for cultural understanding and acknowledgment is highlighted several times, addressing a lack of professional recognition and ignorance in this space. The book challenges us to be more inclusive and connected.

Losa reminds us that our lives are woven with many threads — whanau, tikanga, hahi — that form our intrinsic beliefs and behaviours, both good and bad. Like a Phoenix born out of the ashes, she manifested herself as a *Mana Wahine* through pain, suffering, repentance, and resilience.

Maherau Piho-Arona
PIMDAN President Pacific Islands Mt Druitt Action Network

A privilege and pleasure to endorse Wahine Warrior. A beautifully written journal by my dearest wahine warrior, Losa Patterson. This book will resonate with many Pasifika (and non-Pasifika) readers. The heartfelt insights and strategies to heal from trauma will help us all be *'amazing.'* I love that this book is for Pasifika, by Pasifika.

Paula Archibold
TMAP Teach Me About Property Owner-Director | Mentoring Coach

Thank you for having the courage to speak your story and truth. I love the courage, bravery in each journey of your life. I can relate to many of your situations as I was reading it. I was taken back into my own life growing up with my parents. I grew up in a very traditional home. I was pregnant at 18 and was sent away to Darwin. My eldest son was raised by my parents. As I read about your mum's story, I resonated how my mother grieved for her first born. As a young and vulnerable new mother, she faced the heart wrenching reality of her parents claiming him as their own, usurping their role. Reclaiming her son was a hard-fought battle. During his formative years, he was enveloped in love, cherished by his adoring grandparents who lavished attention on him as their first grandchild.

This was very hard for me; I thought my mother was supposed to support me with my relationship with my son. By the time I was 21, I had both my boys and there's so much of your story that triggered me — I felt like I was reading my own story in the same way. I loved your insights and advice which have been incredibly valuable, and I am grateful for your generosity in sharing your knowledge and expertise with me. Thank you for making me feel heard and understood in every way. I truly appreciate it. May your example inspire and encourage others faced with similar difficult situations.

My key takeaways:

- *A wahine warrior endures pain with faith and courage.*
- *She faces challenges with courage while acknowledging the importance of enduring pain as part of the journey toward healing and growth.*
- *She will rise above challenges and inspire others with her courage and kindness.*
- *She recognises the interconnectedness of compassion and love in the journey of healing.*
- *Remember, forgiveness isn't about forgetting what happened or saying it's okay — it's about finding peace within yourself and moving forward.*
- *I was still a 'good girl' trying my best (I too was a good girl trying my best).*
- *Love conquers all; love is essential in being a wahine warrior!*
- *What I've learned in my own journey to healing, even when it's really hard.*

- Love heals it all.
- In the face of life's challenges, love is the gentle force that mends broken hearts, bridges divides, and brings light to the darkest moments.
- It's in the kindness of a friend (like yourself, Losa) the embrace of family (my boys) and the warmth of a loving husband.
- Love empowers us to grow, to forgive, and to find joy even in hardship.
- My mother's words are: 'Love is forever forgiving.'

Aroha Ripley
Business Coach | AR Personal Artist Management

Wahine Warrior is a deeply moving account of Losa's journey, masterfully intertwining her personal experiences with cultural wisdom and professional expertise. Reading her story, I felt inspired and uplifted by the strength and resilience she embodies. Losa's honest sharing of how she faced and overcame life's challenges provides a powerful beacon of hope for anyone navigating their own struggles. This book is a heartfelt celebration of Pasifika strength, offering profound insights on healing past wounds with courage and dignity.

What stands out most is Losa's ability to create a nurturing and supportive space through her words. As a psychotherapist, life coach, and counsellor, she provides invaluable guidance, especially for those healing mother-daughter relationships. The practical advice and emotional support in *Wahine Warrior* give you the tools to mend and deepen these important bonds. Ultimately, *Wahine Warrior* is about honouring where we come from, healing our emotional scars, and striving for a brighter future. Losa's story encourages us to rise from the ashes of our traumas and step confidently into our power as Wahine Warriors. It's a book that will touch your heart and inspire you to embrace your true strength.

Puawai Reupene
Counsellor | Community Leader

Thank you for writing this book. I have the utmost love and respect for your courage as a *'Wahine Warrior'* to fearlessly and candidly tell your life story with such honesty and disarming vulnerability. Having had the privilege of knowing you for many years, as I read through your chapters, it felt like I was truly discovering who you are for the first time.

I loved how you confronted so many of life's challenges within your story and effortlessly wove them into a template of practical solutions for all who have faced similar challenges, assisting them in their transition from a darker mindset to a more expansive and resourceful approach to becoming who they were born to be.

This book was refreshing, at times raw in its portrayal of hard truths yet also simplistic in its wisdom and application. This powerful book will help everyone, especially women, more completely understand their personal power and take full advantage of the opportunities in this life to achieve their true potential in this mortal journey.

Suzanne Utai
Nesian Point Owner-Director | Licensed Social Worker | Psychotherapist

Wahine Warrior by Losa Patterson is an extraordinary testament to the human spirit. With unflinching honesty and raw vulnerability, Losa shares her struggles with trauma and mental health, revealing the resilience that defines her. More than just a memoir, this book is a beacon of hope. Losa offers practical strategies for overcoming hardships, giving readers the tools to navigate their own battles. Her storytelling is filled with wisdom, compassion, and fierce determination that inspire us to rise above our circumstances.

Wahine Warrior celebrates perseverance, the strength in vulnerability, and the courage to embrace cultural identity and family dynamics. Thank you, Losa, for sharing your journey.

Cassie Howes
Psychologist | New Directions for Life Owner-Director

After many tears and much reflective gratitude, I finally found my moment to compose this endorsement. This book is exquisite, for anyone who has dared to own their story and love through it. Losa takes us on a journey of how to listen to the learning in our histories, our families, our culture. As if in quiet conversation, Losa shares so deeply and generously as a woman and as a clinician. This book is a gift to all of us who aspire to be our own warrior.

Jeremy Higgins
Mindset & Performance Coach | Change Strategist | Content Creator

Thank you for writing this. Thank you for being brave enough to break the cycle. Generations will be blessed because of the choices you've made, and those blessings have already started to manifest. The ode to your mother surprised me—in the most graceful way.

This book is a guidebook to forgiveness. Your realization that acceptance isn't forgiveness was compelling. And then the final chapter. The summation. The source. The healing force being Christ. It was a perfect ending to a heart-wrenching story of pain, grief, trauma, and betrayal, transforming into a story of hope, forgiveness, and love.

Some readers may be confronted by this perspective. Some may even be angry. But their anger can only be their own, derived from their own unresolved trauma. This book is a precious gift. A treasure for future generations. It addresses trauma and abuse, but in doing so, weaves light and hope into its fabric, leaving the reader curious and more fully aware of the complexities of the human condition.

It replaces darkness with hope. It replaces grief with wisdom. It creates space for healing. It lays a foundation for growth. I am left yearning to pave the way forward for those who come after. I am inspired to delve into the discomfort of my grief and work through its weight, to harvest the life-enriching gifts of such labour. This book is primarily a story of love and forgiveness. It has deeply touched me and will touch many others who read it.

Mele Tupu
Manager | Community Leader

This book is an insightful portrayal of an individual vividly depicting the patterns of love, honour, hurt, and graceful resilience. It offers a raw account of how one can spread their wings and overcome adversity while navigating challenges in assimilating into a foreign culture far removed from the oceans of the Pacific. It's a heartfelt journey of personal growth.

Epenesa Kamsoo
Lalaga Pasifika Homeschool Co-Founder & Director

If you are after a short but powerful read that navigates through trauma to healing, hope, and fulfilment, *Wahine Warrior* is the book for you.

Seilosa masterfully weaves back and forth through life-shaping events preceding her birth to shocking realisations in the present day that nurture love, hope, purpose, and positive pathways for the generations to follow her.

Don't be fooled by the small size of this book. It can be read in an hour, but Losa employs exceptional brevity to reflect on numerous big themes, including generational trauma and the reclamation of balance and power; the disempowerment of Pasifika identity to assimilate in the diaspora; being 'othered' in both public and private settings; and finally, God and the unequivocal need for forgiveness in the pursuit of holistic healing and renewal.

Wahine Warrior is specifically Losa's work. It is her story as a Christian, Aotearoa-born, proud Pasifika woman and survivor-come-healer of generational trauma. The depth of her reflection and her determination to transmit healing is evident in the layout. The chapters are led with relevant proverbs from Pasifika and Aboriginal cultures. Losa candidly shares her experience, briefly dissects the issues, and then bullet-points strategies to counteract those issues. The chapters are short but loaded. Be prepared.

I didn't even realise I was holding my breath until I arrived at Losa's poem in the penultimate chapter. I exhaled and cried at the entirety of what I had just read. This was followed by a chapter of praise and worship in the context of her suffering and redemption. However, you don't need to be a Christian for this to resonate. Everyone can take something away from this book. It's like we see better after reading it: we see ourselves better, even if we haven't personally experienced major trauma; we see our family and friends better, and our social lens becomes more understanding and determined.

Losa has emerged, from the ashes of trauma, as a Wahine Warrior with God! May her vulnerability and learnings empower compassion and our own healing as well as that of others.

www.ingramcontent.com/pod-product-compliance
Lightning Source LLC
Chambersburg PA
CBHW072208070526
44585CB00015B/1245